P9-DCY-068

HQ
1064
.U5
B288
1998

The Retirement Handbook

How to Maximize Your Assets and Protect Your Quality of Life

Carl W. Battle
Attorney-at-Law

Sponsored by the National Legal Information Services

SOUTHEASTERN COMMUNITY
COLLEGE LIBRARY
WHITEVILLE, NC 28472

Allworth Press
New York

© 1998 Carl W. Battle

All rights reserved. Copyright under Berne Copyright Convention, Universal Copyright Convention, and Pan-American Copyright Convention. No part of this book may be reproduced, stored in a retrieval system, or transmitted in any form, or by any means, electronic, mechanical, photocopying, recording, or otherwise, without prior permission of the publisher.

Published by Allworth Press
An imprint of Allworth Communications
10 East 23rd Street, New York NY 10010

Cover design by Douglas Design Associates, New York, NY

Page composition/typography by Sharp Des!gns, Inc., Lansing, MI

ISBN: 1-880559-96-X

Library of Congress Catalog Card Number: 98-70407

Printed in Canada

CONTENTS

INTRODUCTION

WHAT DO YOU WANT MOST OUT OF LIFE? A SUCCESSFUL CAREER? A close and loving family? Financial security? A sense of purpose? A wonderful retirement? Surely each of us wants all of these things and more to attain happiness and self-fulfillment in life. So much has changed over the past few decades and more changes are inevitable as we approach a new millennium. Americans are growing older and living longer. There are more than 30 million Americans over the age of sixty-five and twice that figure for the number over fifty. In the past two hundred years, America has seen the life expectancy of its population double. A child born today can expect to live to be at least seventy-five and spend nearly twenty years in retirement. It should be easy to see the need to prepare for our increasingly important retirement and golden years.

As you mature, new issues will face you. Your longer life will present special requirements concerning health, independence, finances, retirement, leisure, housing, and many other issues. The normal life-cycle of (1) learning during youth, (2) working and raising a family during adulthood, and (3) retiring during old age will change with new options and opportunities during each stage. It is up to you to use these opportunities as you grow older by being adaptable and by planning ahead for your future.

With each stage in life will come constantly changing foci and interests. Your midlife transition will likely start in your forties and continue into your fifties. You will start to restabilize your choices and lifestyle. You will also seek to create a better fit between the world and yourself. You are likely to take a new look at life ambitions and contemplate career changes. In fact, it may be imperative to change so that your goals can be accomplished.

Around sixty you can expect to go through a mellowing of feelings and relationships. You will develop a greater comfort with yourself and start to define your accomplishments and measurements of success, rather than have others define them for you. You will start to live for yourself at this stage and not primarily for others.

Also in your sixties and beyond you can expect to go through a review of your life. You will come to accept what has transpired in your life and realize that it does have worth and meaning. Self-fulfillment is reached when you come to value yourself and the choices you have made. There is typically an eagerness to share everyday human joys and interactions and your family becomes a very important focal point.

There are several attitudes with which you may embark on your retirement years. You may take a depressing, It's all over, attitude, and be like many retirees who live lonely and unhappy later years. You may also take an attitude of denial, refusing to accept your seniority and forever trying to prove your youthfulness. This attitude can have humiliating and tragic consequences because of your refusal to deal with the physical reality of aging. The best and healthiest attitude in facing retirement is to be realistic, yet optimistic, and face your limitations and potentials. Maximize your assets, minimize your liabilities, and take advantage of your strengths and capabilities. Learn to accept the things in life that you can't change, and strive to change for the better those things that you can.

The sophisticated population of the 1990s through the year 2000 and beyond will continuously explore alternative models of lifestyles and personal success as people are confronted with a wide variety of possibilities. The decline in the amount of time spent working is a major change of our industrialized and computerized society which impacts the quality of our lives before and after retirement. Today, the average American spends only about 14 percent of his or her life working compared with about 40 percent for early agrarian cultures. This leisure time provides you with the freedom to explore a myriad of recreational, developmental, and professional choices.

With our healthier, longer lives and changing needs and priorities, the way our work and career fit into our lives is also dramatically changing. People are redefining the traditional patterns of work and retirement and reentering the workforce on several occasions during their lifetime. We are also learning the importance of enjoying our leisure time well before retirement. Even our attitude toward retirement is changing, because our perception of retirement and senior life is changing. We are beginning to look forward to retirement with confidence and excitement.

An important fact to enjoying your retirement will be your financial security. However, financial security does not just happen. It requires planning, commitment, and money. Although Social Security provides some basic benefits, your financial independence in your retirement years will likely come from your pension, savings, investments, and other private financial resources. For an independent and fulfilling life you will need to set financial goals and work to achieve them. You will also need to be knowledgeable about your pension benefits, Social Security entitlements, and other sources of assistance.

As a retiree, you will continue to face many of the same issues you have in the past, plus many more, such as pension rights, Social Security benefits, Medicare and Medicaid, health care, elderly housing, estate planning, making a will, disability, credit, consumer protection, and taxes. You will be impacted greatly by increasing medical costs, economic conditions, crime, consumer fraud, and other societal ills.

For a new retiree, dealing with everyday life can be like starting over. You must find the right place to live, make new friends and contacts, develop new skills, and perhaps start a new job. You may have special therapy, transportation, and personal care needs. Emotional and psychological support are also essential. You will also need to keep a position of value and respect in your community to maintain your well-being and a healthy attitude.

Although planning ahead is the best way to an independent and fulfilling retirement, many of us do not take the time to do the things necessary to prepare for retirement. Now, if not sooner, is the time to do the thinking and acting for achieving financial security and for managing difficult choices and crisis situations in the years ahead. Act now, before you are limited by physical disability or mental incapacity from providing for or making decisions for yourself.

Ensure that, if ever you cannot make decisions for yourself, others will represent your wishes, preferences, and best interests. Designating a person to make decisions for you, through a power of attorney or medical directive, may help to avoid lengthy and costly court proceedings to establish guardianship. Put your wishes and decisions in writing to decrease the chances of future mismanagement and mistreatment. Prepare your will now if you have not already done so. A will can provide a good inventory of your property and clear instructions on how you want your property distributed. Look at a living trust, wherein you transfer property to yourself or someone else as trustee, if you are interested in a quicker alternative to probate.

The staggering problem of access to health care in America has generated a lot of public attention over the past few years. Over 40 million Americans lack health insurance. One-third of the U.S. population with incomes below the poverty level do not even qualify for Medicaid. While nearly 98 percent of older Americans are enrolled in Medicare, most remain unprotected against the catastrophic costs of long-term care and medication.

Review your medical and life insurance needs routinely. Decide if whole, term, or some other variant of life insurance is best for you. Pay careful attention to your investments and estate planning strategies to maximize benefits for you and your loved ones. Maintain good credit references and learn how to verify and correct your credit rating.

Many resources are available to retirees to foster self-reliance and fulfillment. These include senior centers, special housing, nursing and meal services, family service agencies, agencies on aging, retirement associations, community centers, churches, and others. Senior organizations and advocacy groups are valuable sources of information for retirees and an avenue of social and political influence for senior citizens.

It is never too early to start planning for retirement. The sooner you start, the more time you will have to set your goals and explore your options. *The Retirement Handbook* has been compiled as a resource to help you address the problems and opportunities you will face during your "golden years." While in some complex situations you may need to consult a legal or financial professional, in all cases, *The Retirement Handbook* will offer guidance as you develop your strategies for an independent and fulfilled retirement.

CHAPTER 1

Staying Independent During Retirement

EVERYONE WANTS AN INDEPENDENT LIFESTYLE AFTER HE OR SHE retires. You want the financial, scheduling, health and emotional freedom to enjoy retirement years that are fulfilling and rewarding. After all, you have worked hard all your life, put in the long hours, and travelled on business during many holidays. Without question, retirement is the only time in your adult life when you are free from the pressures of work and can truly be independent.

Keep in mind at all times that the basis for a happy and independent retirement is a life lived to the fullest. Your retirement years should be ones of peace and comfort spent in close, endearing relationships with family and friends. They should be a time for engaging in rewarding and satisfying activities and endeavors, and a time for helping others and sharing your knowledge and wisdom. They should also be a time for travel, adventure, self-development, and personal enrichment.

But independence during retirement requires preparation long before you retire. As early as possible during your career you should consider your retirement needs and take the steps necessary to attain them.

How to Attain Independence

Taking control of your money, credit, insurance, health, and other resources is fundamental to your independence and overall well-being. The most important step to attaining independence is getting started. For many people, the problem is simply procrastination. People generally do not plan until a major situation has developed. This type of crisis planning is the least effective and it is unlikely to lead to personal independence.

At least ten years before you plan to retire, preferably much sooner, you should sit down and determine your retirement needs. An independent retirement can be expensive, and financial experts estimate that you will need about 70 to 80 percent of your preretirement income to maintain your standard of living during retirement. For the average retiree, Social Security will pay only about 40 percent of preretirement earnings. If your present financial situation will not provide an adequate level of retirement income, you will need to make adjustments in your savings, spending, or income to make up for any deficiencies.

It is up to you to make your retirement dreams come true by setting and attaining financial goals. You should review your financial status on a regular basis by determining your net worth and analyzing how your assets are allocated. You should prepare a budget to keep track of your cash inflows and outflows. Set adequate and achievable goals for savings and investments to provide the necessary resources for retirement. You should also do some estate planning to minimize taxes and administrative expenses, and to maximize value for your family, heirs, and other beneficiaries.

You need to decide on your financial priorities for your retirement. Is it important that you have money to travel the world? Buy a sailboat? Leave a large inheritance for your heir? Whatever your priorities, make sure that you will receive the maximum benefits from your pension, investments, Social Security, and other sources. Again, put your financial goals on paper and review them regularly to make sure that you are achieving your objectives. Refer to chapter 2 for discussion on the specific steps in effective financial planning.

Having access to credit can be essential before and during retirement. Credit may be necessary to purchase big-ticket items or meet unexpected or emergency expenses. Establish and maintain a good credit history in your individual name. Refer to chapter 3 for a more comprehensive discussion on how to manage your credit.

You should maintain close contact with family and friends during retirement, and come to rely on them for help when you need it. Don't feel any guilt asking for their help. At the same time be willing to assist others when you can. Remember that family and friends can't always be there for you because of any number of reasons. They may be far away, travelling constantly, overworked, or facing other demands in their lives. This means that you must be realistic in your expectations of others in planning your retirement.

Determining Your Living Arrangements

A major decision affecting retirement is where to live. Staying independent and living at home is unquestionably the preferred living arrangement for most retirees. However, physical, medical, or financial problems can often prevent this from happening. Do you sell your house? Move to a better climate? Relocate close to family? Be sure to analyze the living costs, access to medical care, and the tax consequences of any move you plan to make during retirement.

Before you move, do your research on the new location. Does it provide the various social services and recreational and cultural activities that you might need during retirement? Check on the availability of good medical care, neighborhood safety, transportation, and other features that are important to you. Consider renting for some time before buying a home to make sure you are comfortable with the new surroundings.

Whether you are moving across town or across the country,

there are a number of housing options. These include retirement communities, assisted-living housing, life-care centers, condominiums, apartments, and single-family homes. Many of these options offer savings on housing expenses, freedom from caretaking, opportunities to interact with peers, and a variety of health care and social services. Consider all of the housing alternatives and decide on the one which provides the greatest benefits for your retirement.

Retirement communities provide social benefits because they are populated by people of retirement age. These communities typically limit residents to senior citizens and may have restrictions on guests and pets. Usually, there are several types of housing and a wide range of services and activities available. These can include transportation, recreation, financial services, medical care, security, group dining, and social events. The retirement community lifestyle may appear rigid to many people, but it remains attractive for some retirees.

Assisted-living housing can be a useful arrangement if health considerations or physical limitations prevent you from living alone or performing certain daily activities. This arrangement usually provides private living quarters in an apartment-style setting with support services for physical activities or medical care from staff or other residents. For retirees who require custodial care or constant medical attention, life-care centers may be a housing option. You typically pay an admission fee and a monthly service fee and are guaranteed housing for life.

Condominiums are a popular housing choice for many retirees because they offer a comfortable and convenient living arrangement without the responsibilities of maintenance and upkeep. These apartment-style homes are purchased instead of rented and common areas, such as atriums, courtyards, and hallways, are shared with other residents. A monthly fee is charged for maintenance and other services by the condominium association.

To find out more information about the available housing

options and retirement services contact your library, bookstore, or the various retirement or senior organizations.

Maintaining Your Health

Maintaining good health is always important, but it is especially so in your retirement years. Although most retirees are in good health, many are not and often do not seek treatment for health problems. It is important that you learn to understand the aging process to distinguish between problems that require medical treatment and those that do not need attention.

You will need to establish a close and ongoing relationship with a doctor whom you feel comfortable with and trust and respect. Discuss your complete medical history with your doctor, including any medications you are taking and complications you may have had in the past. Ask him or her for recommendations and information about diet, weight, stress, exercise, medications, therapies, and anything else that you don't understand about your health. Never be embarrassed to discuss your medical and emotional problems with your doctor.

Before you retire, get a thorough medical checkup. Scheduling doctor visits while you're still employed allows you to receive maximum benefits from your health insurance. After retirement, you may have less coverage. If you have to get new or supplemental medical insurance, your coverage will be affected by your current health condition.

Be sure to check on your Medicare eligibility before you retire and before you reach age sixty-five. Phone 1-800-1213 to get a copy of form SSA7004 which requests information from Social Security about your eligibility. If you don't sign up for Medicare at age sixty-five, when you are first eligible for coverage, you have to pay a higher premium for coverage under Part B, which covers costs for doctors, surgeons, outpatient care, and medical supplies.

The best prescription for good health and independence during retirement is following your good judgment and your doctor's advice, and always keeping a positive spirit. You should decide now, while you are in sound physical and mental health, how you would like to handle situations relating to your aging, such as disability, life supporting medical treatment, or mental incapacity. Take the steps now to ensure that your wishes will be carried out. Make a will, write down medical directives, assign power of attorney, and sign organ donor pledges. Explain your decisions to your family and others who may have to carry out your wishes.

FINDING JOY THROUGH TRAVEL AND INNER PEACE

Travel is a very popular and rewarding leisure activity among retirees. Whether in the United States or abroad, travelling can be an experience that brings enrichment, fulfillment, and a sense of independence. Whatever your budget, you can and should make travel a part of your retirement plans. Keep in mind that many airlines, hotels, resorts, and travel agencies offer discounts and vacation packages to seniors, which can make travel affordable and easy to plan.

Millions of senior Americans participate in continuing adult education. This is an excellent avenue for personal development and socialization. A network of several hundred colleges, schools, and other institutions, called Elderhostel, offers low-cost, short-term residential academic programs for older adults. For more information write to Elderhostel at 75 Federal St., Boston, MA 02110, or phone (617) 426-8056. Adult education programs are also sponsored by local public school systems. Investigate these programs to see if they might offer some benefit for you. Take advantage of museums and libraries. These institutions provide opportunities for learning, enrichment, and leisure-time activities.

A major key to happiness is finding inner peace despite the stress of everyday life. You need stress in your life or life would be dull and unexciting. Although stress adds challenges and opportunities, too much stress can seriously effect your physical and mental health. Your challenge in this stress-filled world is to minimize the stress in your life and make it work for you instead of against you.

Although work-related stress may not exist during retirement, stress will still come from physical, mental, and emotional activities that you undertake every day. Stress is so personal that things that may be relaxing to others may be stressful to you. For instance, you may be the type of person who likes being busy and active most of the time. A day of "taking it easy" or "doing nothing" at the beach may make you feel unproductive and frustrated. Yet others may find such days quite relaxing. Find out what you like and relax your way. Oftentimes, too much stress is caused by trying to conform to other people's expectations.

Too much emotional stress can lead to physical illnesses, such as high blood pressure, ulcers, and heart disease. It can also lead to depression, mental illness, and even suicide. Recognizing the early signs of over-stress, and doing something about them, can make a big difference in the quality of your life.

You can relieve some stress in your life through exercise or physical activity. Running, walking, playing golf, or working in your garden are just some of the activities you might try. It also helps to talk to someone about your concerns and worries. Perhaps a friend, family member, or counselor can help you see your problem in a different light. If you feel your problem is serious, you might seek professional help from a psychologist, psychiatrist, social worker, or mental health counselor. Knowing when to ask for help may avoid more serious problems later.

Getting enough rest and eating well will also help you deal with stress. If you are irritable and tense from lack of sleep or if you are not eating correctly, you will have less ability to deal with stressful situations. If stress repeatedly keeps you from sleeping, you should ask your doctor for help. Although you can use prescription or over-the-counter medications to relieve stress temporarily, these do not remove the conditions that caused the stress in the first place. Medications, in fact, may be habit-forming and also may reduce your efficiency, thus creating more stress than they take away. They should be taken only on the advice of your doctor.

The best strategy for avoiding stress is to learn how to relax. Unfortunately, many people try to relax at the same pace that they lead the rest of their lives. For a while, tune out your worries about time, productivity, and "doing right." You will find satisfaction in just being, without striving. Find activities that give you pleasure and that are good for your mental and physical well-being. Forget about always winning. Focus on relaxation, enjoyment, and health.

One way to keep from getting bored, sad, and lonely during retirement is to go where things are happening. Sitting alone can make you feel frustrated. Instead of feeling sorry for yourself, get involved and become a participant. Offer your services in neighborhood or volunteer organizations. Help yourself by helping other people. Get involved in the world and the people around you, and you will find they will be attracted to you. You will be on your way to making new friends and enjoying new activities.

Your retirement years will be fulfilling if you always look forward, plan ahead, value relationships, take good care of yourself, and maintain a healthy attitude. Your retirement years can be the time for exploring new professional, social, and cultural interests; reestablishing old friendships; enjoying travel and true leisure; and attaining real self-fulfillment. Retirement can be the time of your life.

CHAPTER 2

Achieving Effective Financial and Estate Planning

UNLESS YOU ARE INDEPENDENTLY WEALTHY, YOU WILL INVARIABLY have some concerns during your lifetime over money and finances. In fact, even the wealthy must deal with the issue of money management or their fortunes may be easily lost. It is especially important for those preparing for their retirement years to do effective financial planning.

So many of your dreams will depend on financial security—a home, college for the kids, vacation, a happy retirement. It is up to you to make these dreams come true by setting and attaining financial goals. Review your financial status on a regular basis by determining your net worth and analyzing how your assets are allocated. Prepare a budget to keep track of your cash inflows and outflows. Set realistic, yet aggressive, goals for savings and investments to provide resources for emergencies and retirement. Do some estate planning to minimize taxes and administrative expenses, and to maximize value for your family, heirs, and other beneficiaries. Take steps as early as possible to lay down a financial foundation on which you can build a secure future.

SETTING FINANCIAL GOALS

Setting goals and objectives is critical for an effective financial plan. Start by listing and prioritizing realistic financial goals to create a working agenda. These goals should be revised periodically as conditions, needs, and other developments occur.

Some common financial goals are:

- Reducing personal debt
- Providing adequate retirement income
- Attaining financial security and independence

Reducing personal debt: Debt consolidation and reduction is perhaps one of the most important financial goals. With the elimination of the tax deductibility of consumer debt, credit card and other personal debt becomes a substantial drain on a person's cash. Most individuals get trapped in the spiral of just paying off interest and not the principal balances of these accounts. This allows the interest and principal to continue the compounding process. Although savings and certificate of deposit rates have fallen tremendously, the major credit cards are still charging in excess of 15 to 18 percent. These high consumer interest rates can spell disaster for financial planning and security.

You need to look at ways to control your personal debt by minimizing use of credit cards and consumer credit. You should try to pay cash for most of your purchases if possible. You need to avoid impulse buying because it can wreck your financial planning. Is too much being spent on gifts? Entertainment and dining out? Vacations? Clothing? Although you should enjoy life, finding ways to curb your spending can help you in saving, investing, and meeting your financial goals.

Learning to use the equity on your home can help you manage your credit and advance your financial plans. Unlike consumer interest, home mortgage and home equity interest are tax deductible. Consider getting a home equity loan to pay off consumer loans and consolidate debt. It will likely save taxes and interest in the long run. Various options are available for handling your real estate for maximum benefit, such as reverse mortgages, gifting, and others.

Providing adequate retirement income: Although Social Security provides some basic benefits, your financial independence during retirement will likely come from your pensions, savings, investments, and other financial resources. This means that now more than ever you will be responsible for providing for your own retirement.

As mentioned earlier, during retirement you will need approximately 80 percent of your preretirement income to maintain your standard of living. A major part of your retirement income will likely be the result of your personal savings and investments. Don't forget the importance of your employer sponsored 401(k) plan in saving for your retirement, and use your 401(k) to maximize your financial benefits. You should try to contribute as much money as possible to your 401(k) plan. The earnings that you save are usually tax deferred, and many employers match the 401(k) contribution. Also, you can typically borrow money from your 401(k) at below market interest rates and the interest is tax-deferred income to you. You can advantageously use your 401(k) loans to pay off credit cards and other consumer debts.

Use the retirement planning chart below to set financial goals for retirement:

	YOUR RETIREMENT NEEDS
1. Annual income needed when you retire (80% of pre-retirement income).	$ ________
2. Probable Social Security and pension benefits. Refer to the "Projected annual Social Security benefits" chart below. Add to that figure what your employee benefits counselor estimated your annual pension will be in today's dollars.	$ ________
3. Annual retirement income needed from investments (line 1 minus line 2).	$ ________

4. Amount you must save before retirement (line 3 times factor A below). $ ________
5. Amount you have saved already, including IRAs, corporate savings plans, and other investments. $ ________
6. Projected value of your current retirement savings at the time you retire (line 5 times factor B). $ ________
7. Amount of retirement capital still needed (line 4 minus line 6). $ ________
8. Annual savings needed to reach your goal (line 7 times factor C). $ ________
9. Total you should save each year (line 9 minus annual employer contributions to savings plan). $ ________

Projected Annual Social Security Benefits

WORKER'S AGE IN 1996		WORKER'S EARNINGS IN 1995			
		$30,000	$40,000	$50,000	$61,200+
45	Worker	$12,636	$14,412	$15,912	$17,484
	Worker with spouse	18,948	21,612	23,868	26,220
55	Worker	$12,636	$14,304	$15,444	$16,428
	Worker with spouse	18,948	21,456	23,160	24,636
65	Worker	$12,564	$13,812	$14,532	$14,976
	Worker with spouse	18,840	20,712	21,792	22,464

Source: Social Security Administration, 1996

NOTE: The accuracy of these estimates depends on the pattern of your actual past earnings and on your earnings in the future. Call or visit your Social Security Office to ask for your Personal Earnings and Benefit Estimate Statement.

AGE AT RETIREMENT	FACTOR A
55	23.3
56	22.9
57	22.6
58	22.2
59	21.8
60	21.4

YEARS FROM RETIREMENT	FACTOR B	FACTOR C
5	1.15	0.188
7	1.22	0.131
9	1.29	0.099
11	1.36	0.079
13	1.44	0.065
15	1.53	0.054

61	21.0	20	1.76	0.038
62	20.5	25	2.02	0.028
63	20.1	30	2.33	0.022
64	19.6			
65	19.2			
66	18.7			
67	18.2			

The factors listed above assume a hypothetical 8 percent total return and a 5 percent rate of inflation.

Attaining financial security and independence: The definition of financial security will be different for each of us. Your goal of financial security may be creating a portfolio of $500,000 in marketable securities which will allow you to live off the interest and dividends. It may be having a cushion of one year's salary to protect you in case of unemployment or an emergency.

Whatever your idea of financial security and independence, a good financial planner can be helpful in analyzing your finances and recommending how to improve your financial situation. He or she can assist in preparing a financial plan based on your personal history and financial goals. Before selecting a financial planner be sure to investigate his or her background and experience. For further information on financial planners contact the following organizations:

- National Association of Personal Financial Advisors, 1130 Lake Cook Road, Suite 105, Buffalo Grove, IL 60089; 1-800-366-2732
- Institute of Certified Financial Planners, 7600 E. Eastman Avenue, Suite 301, Denver, CO 80231; (300) 751-7600
- International Association for Financial Planning, 2 Concourse Parkway, Suite 800, Atlanta, GA 30328; (404) 395-1605
- Securities and Exchange Commission, Office of Filings, Information, and Consumer Services, 450 5th Street, N.W., Washington, DC 20549; (202) 272-5624

A successful strategy for maximizing your financial security should comprise (1) controlling your personal debt and expenditures, (2) saving regularly, (3) taking full advantage of tax-deferred and tax-free income plans, and (4) maintaining a diversified and risk-balanced investment portfolio.

Your investment strategy should be one of prudent risk-taking. With most investments, the greater risks usually provide the potential for a greater return to you. However, your level of risk taking typically changes over the various cycles of your life. At a younger age you can afford to take greater risk as you strive to build up your investment assets. When you approach retirement, your risk factor should decline as you focus on minimizing losses and preserving asset value. To help reduce overall risk of loss, your investment portfolio should always be diversified into a variety of investment vehicles.

Cash Flow Management

Managing your disposable income is critical in allowing you to reach your financial goals and objectives. A starting point is to establish a workable budget using the cash flow worksheet below.

Preparing a budget helps you keep track of where your money is going. It also helps in predicting how you will spend money in the future. Budgeting is an important process in setting financial goals and making sure that you are taking the right steps toward meeting them. Start by listing all your sources of monthly income such as salary and wages, pension, annuities, Social Security, interest, dividends, rental income, gifts, and any other money that you receive. Then itemize all of your monthly expenses and expenditures including mortgage, rent, taxes, utilities, insurance, repairs, loans and credit card payments, food, clothing, transportation, recreation, and the like. A helpful exercise is to make journal entries on all cash expenditures on a daily and weekly basis.

Once all the major categories are identified, it is critical to establish spending guidelines for all areas. Subtracting expenses from income gives the disposable income to use for savings and investments. Ideally, your income should be more than your expenses and expenditures, especially during your preretirement years, to allow for savings.

	CASH FLOW WORKSHEET	PER MONTH
INCOME	Wages, salary, and commissions	$ ________
	Dividends, interest, and capital gains	$ ________
	Annuities, pensions, and Social Security	$ ________
	Death benefits from estate	$ ________
	Income on real property	$ ________
	Other	$ ________
	Total income	$ ________
EXPENSES	Taxes	$ ________
	Mortgage/rent	$ ________
	Medical expenses	$ ________
	Utilities	$ ________
	Telephone	$ ________
	Car	$ ________
	Clothing	$ ________
	Childcare	$ ________
	Tuition or education expenses	$ ________
	Insurance premiums	$ ________
	Maintenance of home	$ ________
	Maintenance of car	$ ________
	Hobbies	$ ________
	Entertainment	$ ________
	Vacations	$ ________
	Memberships/professional fees	$ ________
	Gifts and donations	$ ________
	Loans and credit cards	$ ________
	Other	$ ________
	Total expenses	$ ________
	Total income	$ ________
	(minus) Total expenses	$ ________
	Total available for savings/investments	$ ________

DETERMINING YOUR NET WORTH

Determining your net worth periodically lets you know where you are financially. Net worth is calculated by totalling all of the assets and subtracting all of the debts and other liabilities. You can start with the preparation of a net worth statement by listing all of your assets and their value. This should include cash, checking, and savings accounts, certificates of deposits, stocks, bonds, IRA accounts, life insurance cash values, real estate, automobiles, and personal property. Next, you list all of your liabilities, including mortgages, personal loans, credit cards, taxes, and any other debts. The sum of your assets minus your liabilities will tell you how much you are worth.

Use the worksheet below to calculate your net worth:

	CURRENT VALUE		LIABILITIES
LIQUID ASSETS			
Checking accounts	______	Credit card balances	______
Savings accounts	______		______
Money market funds	______	Education loans	______
Cash value of life insurance	______		
Other liquid assets	______	Car loans	______
	______	Personal installment loans	______
Total liquid assets	______	Other loans	______
INVESTMENT ASSETS			
Mutual funds	______	Mortgage	______
Stocks	______	Other liabilities	______
Bonds	______		______
Certificates of deposit	______		______
Other investment assets	______		______
Total investment assets	______		______

RETIREMENT PLANS			
IRA	______		______
401(k) plan	______		______
Company pension	______		______
Other retirement plan(s)	______		______
Total retirement plan assets	______	*Total liabilities*	______
PERSONAL ASSETS	______	NET WORTH	
Residence	______	*Total assets*	______
Vacation property	______	*Minus total liabilities*	______
Jewelry/art/antiques	______	*Your personal net worth*	______
	______		
Total personal assets	______		
Total assets	______		

YOUR INVESTMENT OPTIONS

There are a myriad of savings and investment vehicles available for both short-term and long-term financial goals. These include everything from the simple savings account with banks, credit unions, and savings and loans associations to U.S. Government securities, corporate and municipal bonds, mutual funds, annuities, stocks, real estate, and commodities. An effective investment strategy is to balance risks, yields, taxes, inflation, and liquidity with the best mix of investment channels.

Financial planners have various investing guidelines depending on your age and investment horizons. One example is: subtract your age from one hundred—that number could represent the percentage of assets that should be in stock. However, to help reduce overall risk of loss, an investment portfolio should always be diversified into a variety of investment vehicles.

The U.S. Government offers securities which are very safe with guaranteed rates of return. Treasury bills are issued for periods of thirteen, twenty-six, or fifty-two weeks and are redeemable for the face amount. You pay a discounted amount, and the yield over the time period of the bills is the difference between the face value and the discounted price. You can purchase treasury bills directly from your local federal reserve bank without paying any fees or through an intermediary bank or broker.

The U.S. Treasury also offers EE and Series HH savings bonds. EE bonds mature in twelve years and guarantee a minimum 6 percent rate. If held for five years or longer you will typically earn a competitive market-based rate on EE bonds. You purchase EE bonds at a discounted price and receive the face value of the bond on maturity. The interest you earn on EE bonds is exempt from state and local income taxes, and you pay no federal taxes on the interest income until you cash in the bonds. Series HH bonds are also exempt from state and local taxes and earn 6 percent annual interest which is paid semiannually. The EE and HH savings bonds are very safe investments and can usually be purchased through banks and other financial institutions, or your employer by payroll deduction.

Municipal bonds are another relatively safe investment vehicle. Although their yields are usually lower than riskier investments, the interest earned is typically exempt from federal, state, and local taxes. Municipal bonds can be a useful investment medium if you are in a high tax bracket.

Corporate bonds are an additional investment medium which can offer attractive yields at relatively low to medium risks, depending on the financial health of the issuing company and its bond rating. Bonds with the highest grade are rated as "AAA," and these typically offer a lower yield than the lower-grade bonds. Corporate bonds are usually issued from one to thirty years and are redeemable for the face value at maturity. You purchase the bonds at a discounted price that fluctuates according to market conditions.

You are probably already familiar with the savings plans offered by your bank, such as the traditional passbook savings account. Banks also offer certificates of deposit with varying maturity periods and interest rates. There are usually penalties for early withdrawal of funds from certificates of deposit. Money market accounts are also available at most banks and generally earn a higher yield than your passbook savings account. The money market accounts may provide check writing and other privileges, and may be subject to minimum balance requirements and administrative fees. Your accounts with federally insured banks and credit unions are insured up to $100,000 per depositor.

Annuities from insurance companies or other financial establishments are investment vehicles which guarantee a fixed income for life or a specified number of years. If you want a guaranteed income without having to worry about managing assets to attain it, then you should consider purchasing an annuity. The interest is usually tax-deferred until you make withdrawals. Annuities are only as good as the company issuing them, so be sure to investigate the financial health of the company before purchasing an annuity.

Riskier investments include equity or ownership vehicles such as stocks, mutual funds, commodities, and real estate. When you purchase stock, you are buying part ownership in a company. The value of your stock will go up and down depending on the financial performance of the company and other economic conditions. The stock may also pay dividends determined by company profits. Regular ownership in a company is evidenced by common stock which has no guaranteed rate of return; in fact, the return can be negative. Preferred stock usually offers a specified dividend rate and is paid off before common stock if the company dissolves. Historically, stocks have outperformed most other financial assets such as bonds, money markets, and metals. Over a twenty-year horizon a stock portfolio, on average, will likely generate the most growth and help keep assets constant with inflation.

Mutual funds are a mechanism for you to pool your assets with other investors for investing in a variety of vehicles. Some mutual funds can be speculative and extremely risky and others can be conservative depending on how the fund makes investments. It is very important that you evaluate a fund's historical performance and financial stability before investing in mutual funds.

Real estate and commodities are purely speculative investments and involve a lot of risk. With these investments you are gambling on the future value of assets such as real property, precious metals, foreign currencies, and feed stocks. Always obtain professional advice before investing in high-risk ventures.

SELECTING A FINANCIAL INSTITUTION

Here are some helpful tips from the U.S. Office of Consumer Affairs for choosing a financial institution for checking, saving, and other financial needs. Keep in mind that a good banker can be just as important before and after retirement as a good doctor or lawyer.

Finding the right bank, savings and loan, or credit union means figuring out your own needs first. Answering the following questions should help you identify your "banking personality" and make choosing a financial institution a bit easier.

- What is your goal in establishing a banking relationship? Answers might include "to save money," "to have a checking account," "to get a loan," or all of the above.
- How much money can you keep on deposit each month and how many checks will you write? Knowing this will help you judge how complex or simple an account you need.
- Will you be buying a home or car or making another large purchase in the near future? If so, you'll want to find out about the types of loans offered by the institutions you are considering.
- If you hope to save for a big expense or toward your retirement, you'll also want to find out how many different savings programs are offered.
- What time of day do you prefer to do your banking? Do you like the convenience of automated teller machines (ATMs) or

do you prefer to deal with live tellers? Answering these two questions will help you determine if you'd be happier at a financial institution with regular, evening, or weekend hours, or one with a wide network of ATMs.

- What does the financial institution charge for services like cashier's checks, safe deposit boxes, and stop payment orders? Is there a charge for using an automated teller machine? Is there a monthly service charge, or must you maintain a minimum balance in your account to avoid a charge?

After answering the above questions, you should now be ready to narrow your options to specific financial institutions. You should phone or visit several near your home or office because they are likely to be the most convenient. You can take your answers to the above questions with you and find out which accounts and services are most likely to match your needs. You can then compare fees and service charges, as well as deposit and loan interest rates.

Price might not be the most important factor in your "banking personality," so you should also take a minute to think about how comfortable you feel at each institution. For example, are questions answered quickly and accurately? Do customer service personnel offer helpful suggestions?

Remember, you can choose more than one financial institution to provide you with different banking services. Before making a final choice, make sure the institutions being considered are federally insured. This means deposits will be protected up to $100,000.

Effective Estate Planning

The pen is mightier than the sword—particularly when it comes to estate planning. If you take the time to put pen to paper and plan your estate, you can save a significant portion of your wealth for your family and other heirs. Without proper planning, your estate will be exposed to taxes, probate, and legal fees, and may be significantly depleted leaving little or nothing for your family or heirs. In the absence of a clear plan, there may be disputes about the distribution of your assets, resulting in a waste of time and additional legal and administrative fees. With planning, you can determine the value of your estate and make decisions while you are alive that will preserve it for your heirs later. Through the use of various tools of estate planning, like charitable trusts, living trusts, and life insurance you may be able to avoid some tremendous costs to your estate.

An estate plan is normally used to preserve your estate today and minimize the cost associated with dividing and transferring the value to your heirs later. The plan should also consider ways to accomplish other goals you have for assets that you have accumulated during a lifetime. If your estate plan costs you more than it saves, it is an ineffective plan. Your estate plan should take into account the following costs:

- Appraisals
- Tax filing costs
- Probate fees
- Legal fees
- Auction fees
- Estate taxes
- Administrative fees

To the extent that you can minimize or eliminate these costs, you will preserve more of your estate's value for your heirs.

There are two provisions in the tax law that determine the amount that may be passed to heirs without incurring estate taxes. The first is that when an estate is left to a surviving spouse, regardless of size, there is no estate tax due. The amount that may be passed to a spouse at death is unlimited. This is the unlimited marital deduction.

The second provision involves the Unified Credit, which pertains to amounts passed to other heirs. Currently, the tax law allows for a credit that is equivalent to the tax due on $625,000 of assets. Therefore if you die with an estate of $625,000 or less, there would be no estate taxes due, in most cases. A married couple may leave $1,250,000 to heirs since they are entitled to two unified credits.

Note that in many cases one of the unified credits is lost at the death of the first spouse unless the couple take steps necessary to preserve that credit. Remember, as long as money passes to one spouse there are no estate taxes because of the unlimited marital deduction. But, upon the death of the second, taxes will be due on any amount over $625,000. One basic element of estate planning for married couples should be preserving both unified credits. Working with a good estate planner can help you maximize benefits under the tax laws.

The key to estate planning is establishing goals. Prior to deciding on use of estate planning devices such as a will or various trusts, you should decide what you would like to accomplish with your estate. Is preservation for your heirs important? Would you like to maximize the value to you now or your heirs later? Are you willing to sacrifice a portion of what you have today to leave more for others later? Would you consider gifting assets to charity? Don't get lost in the details on the type of trusts or wills needed because these are merely tools to be used to accomplish the objectives. Rather than thinking about the how and what kind of will or trust, think of the why. Let the professionals worry about how to put your wishes into proper form. Tell your estate planner or attorney what you want accomplished so he can help you accomplish your goals.

There is cost involved in setting up an estate plan. However, by investing money and time today, you may be saving your heirs not only thousands of dollars but also legal and emotional distress later.

Checklist for Setting Up An Estate Plan

- Determine the current value of your estate. Include all assets plus the death benefit from insurance on your life if you are also the owner of the policy. Include cash value of policies that you own even if you are not the insured.
- Set goals; what would you like to accomplish with your

assets? Do you want to preserve the full value for relatives, charity, or others? Any specific bequests (the family heirloom to your daughter)? Any special needs that should be addressed, like providing for the care of a minor or handicapped heir?

- Evaluate your present situation. What costs would be incurred if your estate were settled today, and how would assets be distributed to heirs? Do you have a current will? Does it reflect your true wishes? Make an itemized list of costs for settling your estate. Include funeral expenses, estate and income taxes, probate and legal fees, and payment of creditors. Will there be a cash shortage in settling the estate? If so, it may be necessary to sell assets to cover the shortage. Oftentimes a forced sale of assets could result in diminished market value. This is your "before" picture. A financial analysis done by a financial planner should accomplish the above. The analysis should also point out the dollars that may be saved by making changes in your present situation.
- Compare your "before" picture with your goals. Are changes desirable? Together with your estate planning professional determine what changes need to be made to accomplish your goals.
- Determine the cost that would be incurred to make changes to your "before" picture.
- Evaluate your "after" picture. How will circumstances differ when changes are in place? What problems will an estate plan solve? Will it eliminate cash shortages? Will there be a change in the value of estate to your heirs? Will asset distribution be correct? Is there a benefit to you today?
- Compare costs versus benefits and make a decision on your course of action. Develop an action plan to complete all necessary steps. Include a time frame to get things done.
- Implement the plan. The best laid plans do not accomplish a thing. If you do not follow through and actually implement the plan, you have wasted time and money.

- Review your plan annually. Since everything changes, laws, value of your estate, your personal preferences, etc., you should establish a time for review of your plan at least once a year.

Since estate planning involves financial and legal issues, it is best done through the coordinated efforts of financial and legal professionals that specialize in the area of estate planning. If your estate is complex you should enlist the help of professionals who can effectively coordinate and use all the available tools to accomplish your goals. Do not make the mistake of using an attorney to do the financial analysis or allowing a financial professional to do your legal work. Use only financial planners or attorneys that have special expertise in estate planning.

ESTATE PLANNING DEVICES

A will and trust arrangement can be used as an effective estate planning device. A will is a set of final instructions showing how you would like your property distributed. See chapter 8 for a more detailed discussion on wills. Although none of us like to think of our own demise and the need for a will, it is a necessary document if you have assets and would like to have these distributed according to your wishes. In the absence of a will, court proceedings may be necessary to determine how your estate should be distributed. Thus, a will should be a part of any estate plan.

A revocable living trust is a legal arrangement to hold property during one's life for the benefit of others at one's death. It may be used jointly with your will. The revocable living trust may be changed at anytime by the grantor (the person who sets up the trust). Assets continue under the control of the grantor. This type of trust is normally set up to avoid the time and costs of probate. See chapter 8 for more discussion on living trusts. An irrevocable trust is another arrangement for holding property and can be useful in estate planning. The irrevocable trust, once established, generally cannot be changed and the grantor gives up control over assets transferred to the trust.

Another estate planning device is the charitable remainder trust which allows gifting of assets to a charity without giving up income from the assets during your lifetime. Assets are placed in trust for the benefit of a charity at the death of the grantor. During the grantor's lifetime, the trust will pay an income to the grantor. The grantor will normally receive an income tax deduction when assets are placed into the trust. The amount of the income tax deduction is calculated using Internal Revenue Service (IRS) guidelines. This type of trust is used to provide income today. It is particularly useful when a sale of highly appreciated assets is involved.

Life insurance can be used as an effective estate planning device to transfer the value of assets to heirs. Since life insurance usually avoids probate and administrative expenses, it is an excellent way to transfer assets. See chapter 4 for a more detailed discussion of life insurance.

Gifting and joint ownership arrangements may also be used as part of an overall estate plan. Each one has its advantages and disadvantages. Prior to using a gifting or joint ownership arrangement make sure you fully understand that this also means giving up control of your assets. You can make gifts to an unlimited number of people or organizations without paying federal gift taxes, provided that these gifts do not exceed $10,000 ($20,000 for married couples) per person each year. No taxes are paid on gifts of any amount between spouses. Because tax and estate laws are constantly changing, always seek the advice of a knowledgeable attorney or estate planner before making gift and estate planning decisions.

CHAPTER 3

MANAGING YOUR CREDIT

AS YOU GROW OLDER YOUR NEED TO MAINTAIN A GOOD CREDIT rating becomes of paramount importance. Furthermore, changes in your life, such as divorce, loss of income, relocation, retirement, education for your children, and loss of a spouse, may all trigger a need for you to obtain credit or review your current credit history. Maintaining a good credit history and establishing sources of credit should always be a part of your financial planning.

BUILDING A GOOD CREDIT HISTORY

Although lenders consider a variety of factors in deciding whether to give you credit, most of them rely heavily on your credit history. So, building a good credit history is essential if you want to be able to borrow money. If you have no reported credit history, it may take time for you to establish credit. Although this problem affects young people more than it does senior citizens, there are a large number of seniors (particularly widows and divorcees) who have not established their own credit.

If you do not have a credit history, you should begin to build one.

If you have a steady income, whether from wages or retirement benefits, and have lived in the same area for at least a year, try applying for credit with a local business, such as a department store. Or you might borrow a small amount from your credit union or the bank where you have checking and savings accounts. A local bank or department store may approve your credit application even if you do not meet the standards of larger creditors. Before you apply for credit, ask whether the creditor reports credit history information to credit bureaus serving your area. Most creditors do, but some do not. If possible, you should try to get credit that will be reported. This builds your credit history.

If you do not have a credit file, you can visit or write your local credit bureau and request that a file be started on you. Most credit reporting agencies will require that you provide them with your identification, your address (last five years), social security number, place of employment, and verification of income. If you do not have employment income, take copies of Social Security, disability, pensions, annuities, alimony, and retirement checks. Remember that, under the law, retirement or disability income must be treated the same way as employment income in determining if credit is to be granted. If you have prior creditors, contact them to obtain copies of your last credit transactions. Also, if you have a bank account, attempt to get a letter of reference from your banker and submit these to the credit reporting agency.

Open checking and savings accounts at several financial institutions if you do not have any. These may be useful as credit references and as easier sources of credit because of your ongoing relationship. Most creditors will not extend you credit unless you have at least three good credit references. Apply for a major credit card. If you do not qualify, check to see if you can offer collateral or have someone cosign.

The Federal Trade Commission enforces a number of federal credit laws and provides free brochures and publications on many credit-related issues. The Federal Reserve System and the Federal Deposit Insurance Corporation also provide free consumer pamphlets and handbooks on a variety of credit topics. Much of the following information was provided by these sources.

How Credit Bureaus Work

Credit reporting agencies, often called credit bureaus, are companies that gather information on credit users and sell that information in the form of credit reports to credit grantors, such as banks, finance companies, and retailers. Credit bureaus keep records of consumers' debts and how regularly these debts are repaid. They gather information from creditors who send computer tapes or other payment data to credit bureaus, usually on a monthly basis, showing what each account holder owes or has paid. The data show if payments are up-to-date or overdue, and if any action has been taken to collect overdue bills. The credit bureau adds this data to existing information in consumer files, creating a month-by-month history of activity on consumer accounts.

If you have been denied credit because of information that was supplied by a credit bureau, the Fair Credit Reporting Act requires the creditor to give you the name and address of the credit bureau that supplied the information. If you contact that bureau to learn what is in your file within thirty days of receiving a denial notice, the information is free. If not, the credit bureau may charge you a small fee (i.e., $10–$30).

You always are entitled to learn what is in your credit file, but credit bureaus vary in how they disclose this information. Most will send you a printed copy of your credit report. Some, however, will ask you to visit the bureau to review your record or will give you information over the telephone once you have provided proper identification.

Once you have received your credit report, make sure that you understand the report. Often, credit reports are computer coded for recordkeeping purposes, making them difficult to understand. If you do not understand your report, the credit bureau is required by law to give you an explanation of what your report says. If you still do not understand, you can set up an appointment with a credit counselor to discuss your report.

How to Conduct Your Own Credit Checkup

Even if you have not been denied credit, you may wish to find out what information is in your credit file. Some financial advisors suggest that consumers review their credit reports every three or four years to check for inaccuracies or omissions. This could be especially important if you are considering making a major purchase, such as buying a home. Checking in advance on the accuracy of information in your credit file could speed the credit-granting process.

To find which credit bureaus have your file, check the yellow pages under credit bureaus or credit reporting agencies for the phone numbers and addresses of the bureaus near you. The names and addresses of the four major credit reporting agencies are given at the end of this chapter. When you contact them, give all identifying information, such as your full name, Social Security number, current address, former address, and spouse's name (if applicable). Ordinarily, a credit bureau will charge $10 to $40 to give you your credit file information. To get a complete credit picture, ask all local credit bureaus if they maintain a file on you.

If you are married, you and your spouse probably have individual credit files. These files may contain identical or different information, depending on whether you and your spouse have shared or separate accounts. You and your spouse may find it helpful to review and compare your credit histories together.

Credit information on accounts opened before June 1, 1977, that are shared by a husband and wife often are reported only in the husband's name. However, creditors must report the credit history individually, in the name of each spouse, if you ask them to do so. Newer accounts should be reported on an individual basis automatically. If you find this is not the case, write to the creditor and request that the account be reported in both names. This will help both of you build a credit history.

What a Credit Report Covers

Contrary to myth, a credit bureau neither tracks all aspects of your personal life nor evaluates credit applications. Credit bureaus are simply organizations that collect and transmit the following four principal types of information:

- *Identification and employment data:* Your name, birth date, address, Social Security number, employer, and spouse's name are routinely noted. The bureau also may provide other information, such as your employment history, home ownership, income, and previous address, if a creditor requests it.
- *Payment history:* Your account record with various creditors is listed, showing how much credit has been extended and how you have repaid it. Related events, such as referral of an overdue account to a collection agency, may be noted as well.
- *Inquiries:* Credit bureaus are required to maintain a record of all creditors who have requested your credit history within the past six months. They normally include such creditor inquiries in your credit file for at least this long.
- *Public record information:* Events that are a matter of public record and are related to your creditworthiness, such as bankruptcies, foreclosures, or tax liens, may also appear in your report.

How to Correct Errors in Your Credit Report

Your credit file may contain errors that can affect your chances of obtaining credit in the future. Under the Fair Credit Reporting Act, you are entitled to have incomplete or inaccurate information corrected without charge.

If you dispute information in your report, the credit bureau must reinvestigate it within a "reasonable period of time," unless it believes the dispute is "frivolous or irrelevant." To check on the accuracy of a disputed item, the credit bureau will ask the creditor in question what its records show. If the disputed item is on the public record, the credit bureau will check there instead. If a disputed item cannot be verified, the credit bureau must delete it. If an item contains erroneous information, the credit bureau must correct the error. If the item is incomplete, the bureau must complete it. For example, if your file showed accounts that belong to another person, the credit bureau would have to delete them. If it showed that you were late in making payments, but failed to show that you are no longer delinquent, the credit bureau would have to add information to show that your payments are now current. Also, at your request, the credit bureau must send a notice of the correction to any creditor who has checked your file in the past six months.

If the reinvestigation does not resolve your dispute, the Fair Credit Reporting Act permits you to file a statement of up to one hundred words with the credit bureau explaining your side of the story. Employees of the credit bureau often are available to help you word your statement. The credit bureau must include this explanation in your report each time it sends it out.

Your credit file may not contain information on all of the accounts you have with creditors. Although most national department store and all-purpose bank credit card accounts will be included in your file, not all creditors supply information to credit bureaus. For example, some travel-and-entertainment and gasoline card companies, local retailers, and credit unions do not report to credit bureaus.

No one can legally do a credit check on you without your authorization. Moreover, you want to avoid going from one creditor to another within a short period of time applying for credit. Each time that you complete a credit application, a credit report is usually run on you and reported to the credit bureau. Furthermore, sometimes credit checks are run on you without your knowledge, usually by places that offer instant credit, like used car lots and discount stores. If no credit account is opened as a result, then perspective creditors may view all the inquiries as rejections of your application for credit and feel uneasy in extending you credit. If you discover that there are unauthorized or numerous inquiries on your report, you should write a letter to the credit bureau and request that these inquiries be removed.

If you have been told that you were denied credit because of an "insufficient credit file" or "no credit file" and you have accounts with creditors that do not appear in your credit file, you can ask the credit bureau to add this information to future reports. Although they are not required to do so, for a fee many credit bureaus will add other accounts, if verifiable, to your credit file.

HOW TIME AFFECTS YOUR CREDIT REPORT

Under the Fair Credit Reporting Act, credit bureaus can report most negative information for no more than seven years. The seven-year period runs from the date of the last regularly scheduled payment that was made before the account became delinquent unless the creditor later took action on the account, such as charging it off or obtaining a judgment for the amount due. If a creditor took such an action, the seven years would run from the date of that event. For example, if a retailer turned over your past-due account to a collection agency in 1997, a credit bureau may report this event until 2004. You should be aware that if you made a payment after 1997 on this account, your action would not extend the permissible reporting period beyond 2004.

There are exceptions to the seven-year rule. Bankruptcies may be reported for ten years. Also, any negative credit-history information may be reported indefinitely in three circumstances:

- If you apply for $50,000 or more in credit
- If you apply for a life insurance policy with a face amount of $50,000, or more
- If you apply for a job paying $20,000 or more (and the employer requests a credit report in connection with the application)

You can contact the credit bureau if you believe negative

information is being reported beyond the permitted period and ask that it be removed.

What You Can Do if You Have a Poor Credit History

Before creditors will give you credit, they look at how you have paid your bills in the past. Negative information in your credit file may lead creditors to deny you credit. Information that is considered negative includes late payments, repossessions, accounts turned over to a collection agency, charge-offs (accounts viewed as a "loss" by a creditor), judgments, liens, and bankruptcy.

A poor credit history that is accurate cannot be changed. There is nothing that you (or anyone else) can do to require a credit bureau to remove accurate information from your credit report until the reporting period has expired. However, this does not necessarily mean that you will be unable to obtain credit during the period. Because creditors set their own credit-granting standards, not all of them look at your credit history in the same way. Some creditors may look only at more recent years to evaluate you for credit, and they may grant you credit if your bill-paying history has improved. Before applying for credit, it may be useful to contact creditors informally to discuss their credit standards.

If you cannot obtain credit based on your own credit history, you may be able to do so if someone who has a good credit history cosigns a loan for you. This means that the cosigner agrees to pay if you do not. Or you may be able to obtain a small loan or a credit card with a low dollar limit by using your savings account as collateral. If you pay promptly and your creditor reports to a credit bureau, this new information will improve your credit history picture.

How to Deal with Mounting Bills

A sudden illness or the loss of income may make it impossible for you to pay your bills on time. Whatever your situation, if you find that you cannot make your payments, contact your creditors at once. Try to work out a modified payment plan with your creditors that reduces your payments to a more manageable level. If you have paid promptly in the past, they may be willing to work with you. Do not wait until your account is turned over to a debt collector. At that point, the creditor has given up on you. Most creditors do not want to spend time and money to collect delinquent accounts—all they want is their money! Therefore, in most cases, your creditors will be willing to work with you through your crisis. For example, you may want to offer your creditor interest payments on your debt and delay payments on your principal until your condition changes; also, check to see if your debt is covered by a payment protection plan or other insurance that would pay your debt. In some cases you may be able to get your creditor to accept a partial payment as satisfaction in full for your debt. In any event, you want to keep an open dialogue with your creditor keeping him abreast of your situation.

If you do work out a debt-repayment plan, ask your creditors to report your new, smaller payments to the credit bureau as timely. Otherwise, the credit bureau may report these payments as delinquent because you are paying less than the amount agreed to in your original credit agreement.

Automobile loans may present special problems. Most automobile financing agreements permit your creditor to repossess your car any time that you are in default on your payments. No advance notice is required. If your car is repossessed, you may have to pay the full balance due on the loan, as well as towing and storage costs, to get it back. If you cannot do this, the creditor may sell the car. Do not wait until you are in default. Try to solve the problem with your creditor when you realize you will not be able to meet your payments. It may be better to sell the car yourself and pay off your debt. This would avoid the added costs of repossession and a negative entry on your credit report.

WHERE TO FIND LOW-COST HELP

If you cannot resolve your credit problems yourself or need additional assistance, you may want to contact the Consumer Credit Counseling Service (CCCS). This is a nonprofit organization with more than two hundred offices located in forty-four states that counsels indebted consumers. CCCS counselors will try to arrange a repayment plan that is acceptable to you and your creditors. They also will help you set up a realistic budget and plan expenditures. These counseling offices, which are funded by contributions from credit-granting institutions, are offered at little or no cost to consumers. You can find the CCCS office nearest you by checking the white pages of your telephone directory or by sending a self-addressed stamped envelope to: National Foundation for Consumer Credit, 8701 Georgia Ave., Suite 507, Silver Spring, MD 20910; (301) 589-5600.

In addition, nonprofit counseling programs are sometimes operated by universities, military bases, credit unions, and housing authorities. They are likely to charge little or nothing for their assistance. Or, you can check with your local bank or consumer protection office to see if they have a listing of reputable, low-cost financial counseling services.

THE COST OF CREDIT

If you are thinking of borrowing or opening a credit account, your first step should be to figure out how much it will cost you and whether you can afford it. Then you should shop around for the best terms.

Two laws help you compare costs:

- *Truth in Lending* requires creditors to give you certain basic information about the cost of buying on credit or taking out a loan. These "disclosures" can help you shop around for the best deal.
- *Consumer Leasing* disclosures can help you compare the cost

and terms of one lease with another and with the cost and terms of buying for cash or on credit.

Credit costs vary, so you should compare credit prices from different sources. Under Truth in Lending, the creditor must tell you (in writing and before you sign any agreement) the finance charge and the annual percentage rate.

The finance charge is the total dollar amount you pay to use credit. It includes interest costs, and other costs, such as service charges and some credit-related insurance premiums.

HOW AGE AFFECTS YOUR CREDIT

In the past, many older persons have complained about being denied credit just because they were over a certain age. Or when they retired, they often found their credit suddenly cut off or reduced. So the law is very specific about how a person's age may be used in credit decisions.

A creditor may ask your age, but if you are old enough to sign a binding contract (usually eighteen or twenty-one years old depending on state law), a creditor may not do any of the following:

- Turn you down or offer you less credit just because of your age
- Ignore your retirement income in rating your application
- Close your credit account or require you to reapply for it just because you reach a certain age or retire
- Deny you credit or close your account because credit life insurance or other credit-related insurance is not available to persons your age

Creditors may "score" your age in a credit-scoring system, but, if you are sixty-two or older, you must be given at least as many points for age as any person under sixty-two.

Because individuals' financial situations can change at different ages, the law lets creditors consider certain information related to age, such as how long until you retire or how long your income will continue. An older applicant might not qualify for a large loan with a 5 percent down payment on a risky venture, but might qualify for a smaller loan—with a bigger down payment—secured by good collateral. Remember that while declining income may be a handicap if you are older, you can usually offer a solid credit history to your advantage. The creditor has to look at all the facts and apply the usual standards of creditworthiness to your particular situation.

THE MAJOR CREDIT REPORTING AGENCIES

- TRW Credit Information, P.O. Box 74929, Dallas TX 75374; (714) 991-5100. *Pacific Coast, Rocky Mountain, Southwest, New England, and Mid-Atlantic.*
- Trans-Union Credit Information, P.O. Box 7000, North Olmstead, OH 44070; (312) 408-1050. *Pacific Coast, Rocky Mountain, Midwest, and the South.*
- Associated Credit Service, P.O. Box 674422, Houston, TX 77267; (713) 878-1900. *Midwest, Southwest, and Mid-Atlantic.*
- OBI-EQUIFAX, P.O. Box 740241, Atlanta, GA 30374; 1-800-685-1111. *Pacific Coast, Rocky Mountain, the South, and New England.*

CHAPTER 4

Maintaining Good Life Insurance

IS INSURANCE REALLY NECESSARY? THERE IS LIFE INSURANCE, AUTO insurance, home insurance, medical insurance, flood insurance, mortgage insurance, and more. How much of this do you really need?

From a financial perspective insurance serves a necessary function. Few people are prepared financially to handle the risks of a catastrophic loss. If an unexpected loss would cause financial problems for you, your dependents, or others, then insurance might be prudent to cover the potential loss. Also, if your debts exceed your available assets you should consider life insurance or debt insurance to cover the shortage and to avoid creating a financial burden for your family. Your insurance requirements should be reviewed regularly to assure that you are protected against unacceptable financial losses.

What Is Insurance?

Insurance is basically a contract between you and an insurance company which protects you against losses and liabilities. This contract is typically referred to as an insurance policy. The insurance company usually agrees to pay a "benefit" upon the occurrence of a certain event to a designated "beneficiary" in exchange for a "premium." The policy owner may typically name the insured person, place, or event and the beneficiary. The policy usually has a time component, benefits, a premium, and may include other terms governing the relationship between you and the insurance company. The policy, such as a life insurance policy, may include savings, dividends, and special provisions for loans, along with riders that cover special circumstances.

With any insurance, the risk of a devastating financial loss is passed off to an insurance company that has the resources to cover the loss. When considering insurance you should be certain the company you choose has the financial reserves necessary to cover expected losses. Be sure the insurance company is likely to be around with the dollars necessary if you need them. Don't buy insurance from a company that does not have a good reputation and a high rating by BEST, Standard & Poor's, or Moody's agencies.

Every policy has some type of premium—the amount you submit to the insurance company in exchange for the coverage you receive. But premiums vary with the type and amount of insurance and other factors. Some policies, such as whole life insurance, have cash value after a period of time; meaning that they are a form of investment or savings which allows you to get a return over time for some of your premium payments.

Like most financial products, insurance policies cover a wide range. Among the life insurance policies offered are: term, whole life, single-premium life, joint life, second-to-die, and universal or variable life, to name a few. What should you know about insurance in order to make an intelligent choice? Do you need to understand every facet of every available policy? With a basic understanding of the way insurance works and your own financial needs, you will be in a good position to make an intelligent selection.

REVIEWING YOUR LIFE INSURANCE NEEDS

Basically, there are only two types of life insurance, term and cash-value (commonly referred to as whole life). Both types of life insurance will be discussed later. Insurance companies vary these term and cash-value policies and mix the two in single policies to satisfy market demands. As you consider the products on the life insurance market, be aware that life insurance products are tailored to meet specific needs and objectives. If you do not have the time to thoroughly review the market, get a competent, trusted agent who will be concerned about your insurance needs and your financial situation. Try to find an agent who has knowledge of a wide range of products so that he or she will make the best recommendations for your particular circumstances.

There is a wide range of products available when choosing life insurance. Insurance companies are combining investment options and flexibility to create life insurance and investment products for specific groups. With this variety, you should be able to find life insurance that fits your needs and makes sense for your financial situation.

The main reason for having life insurance is usually for the death benefit. Before making a decision on life insurance you should determine what size death benefit is needed to cover all the financial requirements that would result from a premature death.

For your dependents the value of life insurance is obvious—you can create an "instant estate" providing for a surviving spouse and children to the extent that you can afford and desire to do so. When considering life insurance take some time to do the arithmetic. What sort of financial stability would you want to provide for your family or other beneficiary? What type of financial stability do you and your spouse want to provide for each other in the event of a death. Consider things like existing debts, final expenses, and inflation. Do you want to provide for college for children or grandchildren? What about other unexpected expenses?

After selecting the right death benefit, look at the other benefits that may be available from your policy. As with any contract make sure you are getting what you want and make sure you understand your obligation for premium payments; how much and when they are due. Can you skip payments and retain coverage? How many years do premiums continue? Get an understanding of other benefits that you may acquire and what these will cost you.

From a financial perspective, when you buy a life insurance policy you commit yourself to a small regular financial loss in the form of insurance premiums in exchange for coverage in the event of an unexpected death, which could be accompanied by a much larger financial loss. The policy may offer various incentives to soften or lower the financial cost to you. One key incentive may be a savings or dividend component. For these reasons you should stop thinking about premiums only as a cost of insurance. Your premiums can also be an investment and savings mechanism.

One of the advantages of life insurance in general is that the death benefit passes to the beneficiary free of income taxes. The increase in cash value of a whole life policy also accumulates on a tax-deferred basis. However, the death benefit may be subject to death or estate taxes in certain cases.

TYPES OF LIFE INSURANCE

Let's review some of the common types of insurance you might consider and the advantages and disadvantages of each. These include term insurance and cash-value insurance, such as whole life, single-premium whole life, universal life, variable life, first-to-die, and second-to-die.

Term Insurance

A term insurance policy provides life insurance for a specified period of time, such as one year, five years, twenty years, or up to a certain age. In some cases there may be provisions for renewal, but premiums will likely increase upon renewal because you are older. Term policies are "bare bones" policies with few extras. If you will need life insurance for a limited period of time and have limited discretionary income, term life insurance may be your best buy. It may be the only way you can afford the coverage you need at this point. If you can afford more and have a long-term need for life insurance, perhaps something other than term may be better for you.

Generally, if you will need life insurance for more than ten years, it may be to your advantage to consider cash-value policies that offer a savings or investment element. Most term policies expire without ever paying any death benefits. If your insurance needs will extend well into the future, you should be aware of the escalating cost of your term policy. You may reach the point in your older years when the cost of term insurance is out of your reach. Term insurance may be less expensive in the short term, but not in the long term. If you plan to leave a sizable estate to heirs through life insurance, then term policies typically will not be the best choice.

One of the disadvantages of term policies is the termination date. After a specific period of time the term policy will end with no cash value. There are policies available that are guaranteed renewable or that may offer the right to convert the term policy to a cash-value policy. But, in most cases, term policies will expire with no provisions for renewal or conversion. If your circumstances change or you become uninsurable because of health during the period that you are covered by a term policy, you may be unable to find life insurance when you need it most.

The advantages of term life insurance is its simplicity and low cost, in early years. The disadvantages are its termination date, increasing premiums, and lack of cash value and limited tax advantages.

Cash-Value Insurance

Cash-value life insurance will in general include all the available life insurance, except term insurance. Cash-value insurance combines an element of insurance with an investment or savings account. Over time the cash value of the policy should reach or exceed the initial death benefit. There may be good financial reasons for you to choose cash-value insurance, particularly if you have a long-term need for life insurance. As with most long-term investments there may be a longer period of time before you see a good payoff from a cash-value life insurance policy. If you bail out early, you may lose money. However, if your cash-value insurance is properly selected to suit your financial circumstances, the return can be very attractive in the long run.

Cash-value life insurance has basically two components—the cost component and the savings/investment component. The cost component is the portion of your premium that actually pays for your death benefit coverage. Since cash-value policies increase in value as you pay premiums, not all of the premium is used to cover the death benefit. The charge for the death benefit is less than the amount of your premium, resulting in a balance (cash accumulation) in your account that accumulates over time. As your cash accumulates it earns a return which also accumulates in your account.

The cash value in your policy is generally available through loans or surrender of the policy even before the death benefit is payable. Remember that a key advantage gained for earnings on your cash account is its tax-deferred status. If the value in your cash account does not exceed the amount paid in premiums you may avoid taxes on the earnings because these are viewed as a return of premiums. Cash-value insurance policies will typically provide several methods for withdrawing your dollars. The cash value in your insurance policy is usually available quickly and gives you a very liquid asset.

There are typically three ways to get money from your cash-value policy. You may borrow against the cash value of the policy, usually at some interest rate which is below the market rate. If you die before the loan is repaid, the amount owed plus any interest will be subtracted from the death benefits that will be paid to your beneficiary. You may also surrender the policy and the insurance company will pay you the cash value. With surrenders there may be a surrender charge, particularly in the early years of a policy. Make sure that you understand any surrender charges, how you may avoid them, and when surrender charges will not apply. Lastly, you can typically use the cash value of your policy to buy an annuity that provides a guaranteed monthly income for life.

Whole Life

Whole life is one of the most common cash-value policies. Whole life policies have a guaranteed death benefit, guaranteed interest rate, and guaranteed premium over the life of the policy. Generally whole life policies pay a lower rate of interest than other cash-value policies. Whole life policies are usually designed to have the cash value equal to the death benefit when the insured reaches age one hundred.

If you have a short-term insurance need or if your insurance needs are likely to change, a whole life policy may not be best for you. The advantages of whole life are its fixed death benefit, fixed premium, lifetime coverage, tax advantages, and cash value. Its disadvantages are its relative inflexibility, low rate of return, and higher initial cost.

Single-Premium Life Insurance

Single-premium life policies are funded with a lump sum investment. This type of policy will credit interest or dividends to the cash account and deduct insurance costs periodically. Single-premium policies may offer a very attractive return to the long-term investor. In addition to the interest or dividends that you receive on your investment, these earnings will grow tax-deferred as long as the funds stay within the policy.

You may access your cash from a single-premium policy via surrenders or loans. With this type of policy, the IRS has closed some of the tax advantages for contracts purchased after June 21, 1988. Distributions in the form of loans or surrenders will be considered a return of earnings first and an investment last. In some cases there may be a 10 percent tax penalty for distributions made prior to age fifty-nine-and-a-half.

Advantages of single-premium life insurance are its guaranteed return, tax-deferred earnings, and lifetime coverage. The major disadvantage is the large up-front premium.

Universal Life

Universal life policies offer you the advantage of changing many of the key elements of your policy: death benefit, premium amount (within limits), length of coverage, timing of premium payments. Typically you may pay premiums at any time and in any amount. You can also change the amount of your insurance relatively easily. Generally, these types of policies offer a competitive interest rate on your accumulated funds.

Rates are usually guaranteed for one year, and then a new rate is determined subject to a specified minimum rate. You have the option of adding money to your account at any time, thus contributing to a long-term, tax-deferred investment vehicle. If your insurance needs change you may increase or decrease the amount of your coverage without surrendering your policy. However, if you are increasing the death benefit, there may be a requirement to prove insurability again.

You may typically access your cash from these policies via loans or surrenders. The insurance company will probably have charges for surrenders during the early policy years. You must be careful not to exceed IRS guidelines regarding the amount you may invest into these policies to avoid tax liability and penalties. Your insurance agent can help you stay within the IRS limits and avoid tax problems.

The advantages of universal life insurance are its flexible death benefit, flexible premium, lifetime coverage, guaranteed return, and tax-deferred earnings. The disadvantages are its relative complexity, the need for regular review, and investment charges and expenses. Consider universal life if you have a frequently changing need for long-term insurance and savings.

Variable Life

Variable life insurance provides death benefits and cash values that fluctuate, depending on the performance of the investment options that you choose. With variable universal life you will have the opportunity to make decisions regarding the investment of the dollars within your account. Your investment choices usually include stocks, bonds, and money market funds. Although you can realize a higher return with variable life insurance, you also assume the risk of poor investment performance.

The cash value in a variable universal life policy may be accessed through policy surrenders and loans. The policy is subject to IRS rules and regulations on funding and withdrawals. Again, a good agent can help keep you within the guidelines. Agents selling variable life insurance must be registered with the Security and Exchange Commission and licensed by the National Association of Securities Dealers. Your agent should give you a prospectus on any variable life insurance policy that includes an extensive disclosure about the policy.

A variation on variable life policy is variable universal life. The variable universal life may fix the amount of the death benefit and have the value of the accumulation account change with market conditions.

One of the advantages of variable life is that it allows you to choose from a wider range of investment vehicles and integrate your insurance into your overall investment strategy. Other advantages are its lifetime coverage, tax-deferred earnings, and access to cash value. The disadvantages are its relative complexity and investment risks with no guaranteed return.

First-to-Die Policies

First-to-die policies cover two persons and pay a death benefit on the first death of either of the insured. With the two-income family and the financial risk to families at the loss of either wage earner, first-to-die policies offer a method of covering two lives at a lower cost. First-to-die policies are relatively new and are a direct response to the changes resulting from dual-income families.

Second-to-Die Policies

Second-to-die policies cover two people and pay a death benefit on the second death. These policies are generally used in estate planning to replace dollars lost to estate taxes or to provide funds necessary to pay estate taxes due. The policies may also be useful in funding a trust. Because they are based on joint life expectancy, the premiums are usually less than those for two separate single life policies.

TAX TREATMENT OF LIFE INSURANCE

One of the real advantages to investing in life insurance is the favorable tax treatment of distributions from insurance policies. If you are careful about the way you take distributions you may be able to receive your life insurance earnings effectively tax-free. Return of premiums generally are not taxed. Loans against cash values may also avoid taxes. With planning you can effectively withdraw most of the value of your policy through loans and surrenders and avoid any income taxes.

An additional advantage for estate planning may be the death benefit. The death benefit will be paid to your beneficiary and generally will not be subject to income taxes. Although there are a number of methods to obtain the cash value from your life insurance, you should pay careful attention to how you fund the policy and how you take the cash. You should consult your insurance agent or tax advisor to review your specific case and how to comply with IRS regulations. Otherwise, you may be taxed on distributions from your policy first as a return of earnings and may face other tax penalties.

Up until changes were made with the Tax Reform Act of 1986, distributions from insurance policies received extremely favorable tax treatment. The Tax Reform Act restricted distributions on policies issued after December 31, 1984, and provided less favorable tax treatment on the distributions from policies issued after that date. Policies issued between December 31, 1984, and June 21, 1988, may also be subject to the more restrictive regulations, depending on the amount put into the policy and whether you have made material changes to the policy.

If you have a policy issued before December 31, 1984, you are in the best position to use it to generate "tax-free" income. You may be able to take surrenders up to the full amount you have paid into the policy as a return of principal while avoiding taxes all together. For amounts in excess of your payments (earnings) you may take loans, thus effectively allowing you to use your earnings tax-free. Again, if the loans are not repaid they will be deducted from your death benefit.

The Tax Reform Act of 1986 placed restrictions on the accumulation of cash value within a life insurance policy and on the amount that you may add to your policy. There are also restrictions on the number of years the policy must be in force prior to taking distributions. If your policy violated these guidelines it will be classified as a modified endowment contract, and you will lose most of the tax advantages on loans and surrenders. Under a modified endowment contract the distributions will always be viewed as earning first and principal or return of premiums last. If you are under fifty-nine-and-a-half you may also have a tax penalty on distribution. Preventing your insurance policy from being classified as a modified endowment contract is crucial in avoiding the more restrictive tax treatment. Although your policy may not be classified as such initially, this may occur later if you violate the guidelines on cash accumulation and funding. A competent insurance agent, tax advisor, or financial planner can help you meet these guidelines.

Using Life Insurance to Meet Financial Goals

Life insurance policies can be used effectively to accumulate cash for long-term goals. For example, your insurance need may be coupled with a long-term savings need, such as funding retirement. Life insurance can also be used as a means for paying for estate taxes, medical expenses, funeral expenses, and other needs. A cash-value policy offers the best opportunities through life insurance to reach some of your long-range financial goals.

Remember the variety of options that may be available to you. By having a large cash value accumulate within your life insurance policy, you can:

- Purchase an annuity
- Borrow against the total cash value
- Surrender the policy for the full cash value
- Use the policy as a gift or to transfer wealth to your heirs

The first step in utilizing life insurance effectively is to determine your financial needs and the amount of insurance necessary to cover them. Some financial advisors recommend that you should have life insurance equal to five times your total annual earnings. Thus, if your annual income is $50,000, life insurance in the amount of $250,000 is suggested.

However, this general rule may not apply to everyone, because of special circumstances and financial needs. For example, you may want to provide financial stability for your family during retirement for ten years and pay off your mortgage. If annual income is $50,000 and mortgage on your home is $160,000, your life insurance needs can be calculated as follows:

Ten-year income	$ 500,000
Mortgage	160,000
Total need	$660,000

Less:

Retirement and Social Security income	$ 300,000
Current investments	100,000
Employer paid insurance..................................	100,000
	$ 500,000
Life insurance need	$ 160,000

Take time to figure your financial needs, including income needs, mortgage, final expenses, and other debts. Make sure you allow for inflation and subtract present assets that might be used. You can make wise life insurance decisions if you go through a comprehensive review of your responsibilities, financial requirements, and resources. Examine your life insurance needs periodically to take into account changes in family circumstances, living arrangements, and other variables.

Be sure to explain your life insurance coverage to your family and beneficiaries. Give them your agent's name and address and a photocopy of your policy. Your beneficiaries should also know where you keep your life insurance policies. Upon your death, they will need to send copies of your policy and death certificate to your insurance companies in order to get paid.

CHECKLIST FOR BUYING LIFE INSURANCE

- Compute the amount of insurance you need. What amount of financial loss would you like to cover in the event of a premature death? What amount of financial resources have you accumulated to cover the loss?
- Determine the type of policy desired. Do you want cash-value or term? How many years will you need coverage? Do you have a long-term savings need? Is tax deferral on savings important?
- Select a competent and trustworthy insurance agent. Purchase your life insurance from a reputable insurance company.

- Compare various insurance companies, policy options, and costs.
- Read your life insurance policy and make sure that you understand your coverage, exclusions, and other provisions.
- Let your family and beneficiaries know about your life insurance policies and where you keep them.
- Review you life insurance needs and your insurance policies at least annually. Is the beneficiary correct? Should the amount of insurance be increased or decreased? Should you invest additional cash in a policy or take some of the cash value? Does your insurance fit your estate planning needs?

Keeping Good Health Insurance

A major illness or disability can be financially devastating if you don't have adequate health insurance. The problem of access to health care in America has generated a great deal of public attention over the past several years. Over 40 million Americans lack health insurance. One-third of the U.S. population with incomes below the poverty level don't even qualify for Medicaid—a joint federal-state program providing health care for the poor. While nearly 98 percent of older Americans are enrolled in Medicare—a federal health insurance program for people age sixty-five and older—most remain unprotected against the catastrophic cost of long-term care and medication.

Although a national health insurance program has been under consideration, you must ultimately make sure that health care financing is provided for you and your family. You must review your needs for medical insurance coverage and compare the various options. You need to understand what types of coverage you can obtain through employer group insurance, health maintenance organizations, and other private health insurance—as well as Medicaid, Medicare, Veterans Administration, and other government-sponsored health insurance programs. More detailed information on these programs is provided in chapter 5.

Many employers provide group health insurance for their employees. Some plans also offer spousal and family benefits. Some associations and organizations offer similar group health insurance to their members. These group health plans usually pay 80 percent or more of most major medical and hospital costs. There is typically an annual deductible in the range of about $1,000 to $3,000. In many cases, your employer's group health insurance is provided at little or no cost to you. In other cases, it is still substantially cheaper than buying private health insurance on your own, and the costs usually are payroll-deducted.

If you are not covered by a group health insurance plan you will likely need to purchase some type of private health insurance. This will typically be major medical insurance to cover serious illness or injury or Medigap insurance to cover medical expenses which are not picked up by Medicare. Because private health insurance can be relatively expensive, make sure that you maximize the required health insurance coverage you can obtain through Medicaid and group insurance plans.

HOW TO GET GOOD AUTO INSURANCE

With the increasing number of cars on the road, having good auto insurance has become a necessity, and it is required in most states before you can register or operate a motor vehicle. But deciding on the right auto insurance coverage can be quite confusing. Before you order auto insurance, you need to be certain that you understand your basic coverage, what is available for extra protection, what discounts and credits you may qualify for, and what minimum coverage may be required by law.

Your auto insurance basically provides financial protection for damages resulting from your automobile for which you may be held legally liable. The basic coverage should include bodily injury and property damage insurance. Bodily injury protects you in the event you are legally liable for injury to another person as the result of an automobile accident. The first limit is the amount the policy will pay as a result of injury to any one person. The second limit is the maximum amount the policy will pay for injuries to more than one person. A coverage amount of $100,000 to $200,000 is usually adequate. Property damage insurance protects you against financial loss for damage to another's property, if you're legally liable for that damage. A coverage of $50,000 is usually recommended for property damage. These two coverages are the most important part of your auto policy since they protect you against your greatest potential financial losses.

Even if you receive medical benefits from another source, you may want to carry insurance coverage, which provides benefits—regardless of who's at fault in an auto accident—for yourself as well as passengers in your vehicle if you can afford the additional costs. No-fault coverage is optional in some locations and mandatory in others. It typically pays for medical expenses, hospital costs, and rehabilitation costs up to the limit of the policy. It may also include compensation for loss of income to cover part of your salary, essential household expenses, and accidental death benefits.

If your vehicles are financed, your bank or credit union usually requires that you carry coverage for damage to your autos. If your vehicles aren't financed, your decision to carry this coverage should be based on the vehicles' actual cash value and whether you could afford the out-of-pocket loss in the event of an accident.

There are two types of physical damage coverage:

- *Collision* coverage pays you, minus the deductible and subject to your vehicle's depreciation, for damage to your vehicle caused by collision or upset.
- Comprehensive coverage for *damage other than collision* protects you against loss where your car is damaged by something other than collision. It pays you, minus the deductible and subject to your vehicle's depreciation, for damage to your vehicle caused by fire, theft, earthquake, floods, hail, windstorm, vandalism, and other perils not specifically excluded in the policy. Glass breakage is usually also covered.

The insurance rates you pay for your car can vary dramatically depending on the insurance company, agent, or broker you choose, the coverage you request, and the kind of car you drive. Listed below are some helpful tips for lowering auto insurance costs from the Insurance Information Institute, 110 William St., New York, NY 10038.

- Comparison shop. Prices for the same coverage can vary by hundreds of dollars, so it pays to shop around. Ask friends, check the yellow pages, or call the state insurance department. Also check consumer guides and insurance agents or companies. This will give an idea of price ranges and tell which companies or agents have the lowest prices. But don't shop price alone.

  The insurer selected should offer both fair prices and excellent service. Quality personal service may cost a bit more but it provides added conveniences, so talk to a number of insurers to get a feeling for the quality of their service. Ask them about ways to lower costs. Check the financial ratings of the companies too. Then, when the field has been narrowed to three insurers, get price quotes.
- Ask for higher deductibles. Deductibles represent the amount of money a person pays before he makes a claim. By requesting higher deductibles on collision and comprehensive coverage, insurance costs can be lowered substantially. For example, increasing the deductible from $200 to $500 could reduce the collision cost by 15 to 30 percent.
- Drop collision and/or comprehensive coverage on older cars. It may not be cost effective to have collision or comprehensive coverage on cars worth less than $1,000 because any claim would not substantially exceed annual insurance costs and deductible amounts. Auto dealers, credit unions, and banks can provide information on the worth of a car.
- Eliminate duplicate medical coverage. If a person has adequate health insurance, he may be paying for duplicate medical coverage in his auto policy. In some states, eliminating this

coverage could lower the personal injury protection (PIP) cost by up to 40 percent.

- Buy a "low profile" car. Before buying a new or used car, check into insurance costs. Write to the Insurance Institute for Highway Safety, 1005 North Glebe Road, Arlington, VA 22201 and ask for the Highway Loss Data Chart.
- Consider area insurance cost if making a move. Costs tend to be lowest in rural communities and highest in city centers, where there is more traffic congestion.
- Take advantage of low-mileage discounts. Some companies offer discounts to motorists who drive fewer than a predetermined number of miles a year.
- Find out about automatic seat belt or air bag discounts. You may be able to take advantage of discounts on some coverage if you have automatic seat belts and/or air bags.
- Inquire about other discounts. Some insurers offer discounts for more than one car, no accidents in three years, drivers over fifty years of age, driver training courses, antitheft devices, antilock brakes, and good grades for students.

CHAPTER 5

PROVIDING FOR YOUR HEALTH CARE

GOOD HEALTH AND ACCESS TO HEALTH CARE WILL ALWAYS BE important, especially in your retirement years. Yet, increasing hospital costs, doctor's fees, and other medical costs have left tens of millions of Americans without health insurance or the means to pay for adequate health care. In planning for your retirement years, make sure that health care financing is a top priority. Review your needs for medical coverage and compare the various options. Understand what types of coverage you can obtain through Medicare, Medicaid, and private health insurance.

TYPES OF PRIVATE HEALTH INSURANCE

There are many types of private health insurance in the marketplace that will cover some of your medical costs. Descriptions of the most common ones follow.

Major Medical Expense

These policies help provide coverage for the high cost of serious illness or injury, including some health services which may not be covered by Medicare. The primary benefit of a major medical insurance policy is to protect you from the costs of a catastrophic injury or illness. The policies often have a large deductible and they may not cover Medicare's deductibles and coinsurance amounts. Make sure that you thoroughly understand the coverage you will be obtaining before purchasing major medical insurance.

Employer Group Insurance

As mentioned earlier, many employers provide group health insurance for their employees and retirees. Some plans also offer spousal benefits. Even in cases where no medical benefits are provided to retirees, upon your retirement it may be possible to convert your employer group insurance coverage to a suitable individual Medicare-supplement policy when you reach age sixty.

If this is the case with your former employer, carefully compare the benefits and costs of your plan with other supplemental policies. If you switch to another supplemental policy, be sure to continue coverage under your old policy long enough to cover any waiting periods the new policy may have. A waiting period is the time between the date when you become insured and the date when the policy will pay benefits for a preexisting condition or certain other specified illnesses.

Do not drop your policy with your former employer without adequate advice. If the premium is paid by your former employer, or even if a small amount is paid by you, it is sometimes wise to retain the policy and buy a minimum benefit supplemental policy for complete coverage. Contact your employer's personnel office for additional information.

Medigap Insurance

Medigap or Medicare supplement insurance, sold by private insurance companies, is a form of coverage designed to fill the gaps in Medicare protection. Keep in mind that the expenses not covered by Medicare are your financial responsibility. Examples of such expenses include: Medicare deductibles, premiums, any charge above and beyond Medicare-approved limits, coinsurance, and the cost of any service (including most long-term care) or supplies not covered by Medicare. Since these expenses can be substantial, you should consider a Medigap policy for financial protection against noncovered medical care costs.

You should be aware that federal legislation simplifies comparison shopping for any policy held to be, or marketed as, a Medicare supplement policy (the legislation does not apply to employer or union policies). The U.S. Congress, in its legislation, directed the National Association of Insurance Commissioners to design standard Medicare supplement plans, along with standardized (and clearer) language, definitions, and terms. These actions were taken because many consumers were confused by complicated provisions and had difficulty choosing from among the hundreds of policies available to them. As a result of the legislation, there are now ten standard plans, the first of which contains only basic benefits and is designated as "Plan A." In each of the other nine plans, designated as Plans B through J, you would get basic benefits plus one or more additional benefits. Each state is required to implement the federal provisions.

For further information on these plans, consult the *1992 Guide to Health Insurance for People With Medicare* (Publication No. HCFA 02110).

TIPS FOR BUYING PRIVATE HEALTH INSURANCE

The following suggestions will help you in making the best private health insurance decision:

- Comparison shop with respect to coverage and cost. Make a chart that will allow you to see how the different plans compare with respect to such items as deductibles, coinsurance, and prescription drugs.
- Buy only the amount of insurance you reasonably need.
- Look at whether the policy pays a set dollar amount or a percentage of the cost of care. Keep in mind that inflation

causes policies with fixed dollar amounts to lose relative value over time.

- Look at how long the coverage will last.
- Check for waiting periods, preexisting conditions, exclusions, and noncovered medical services, such as treatment of mental illness, alcoholism, or drug addiction.
- Find out how much nursing-home care and home health care cost in your area, in order to determine if policy coverage will be adequate.
- Beware of illegal insurance sales practices! You should not believe anyone who tells you that he or she is from the government and tries to sell you insurance. Medicare supplement policies are not sold or serviced by the Medicare program or any other state or federal government agency. Further, it is illegal for any insurance company or agent to knowingly sell you a policy that duplicates Medicare coverage or your private health plan. Insurance companies or agents that violate this law are subject to federal penalties. Call your state insurance department or the U.S. Department of Health and Human Services at 1-800-638-6833 if you think you have been a victim of an illegal insurance sales practice.
- Do not let a salesperson pressure you. Take the time needed to make an informed decision.
- When you receive your policy, do not delay reading it. Make sure that it provides the coverage you ordered.

Further, the U.S. Senate Special Committee on Aging provides these helpful tips about buying supplemental health insurance.

- Identify Medicare's gap to determine what is important to you in a Medicare supplemental policy. Also consider such policy features as premiums, waiting periods, preexisting condition exclusions, and maximum benefit clauses.
- Take into account any other coverage you have that continues beyond age sixty-five.
- Find out which doctors accept Medicare assignment and are

participating physicians. Lists should be available at your nearest Social Security office or area agency on aging.

- Work with hometown agents and companies that you know. A company must meet certain qualifications to do business in your state. In most states, agents must also be licensed by the state and must carry proof of licensing showing their name and the company they represent. Ask whether they belong to any professional organization so you can check their credentials.
- Talk with your friends who have good experience with the Medigap policies.
- Investigate group insurance sold by legitimate organizations and associations. Some of the senior citizen or retired person organizations are "legitimate" and others are "gimmicks" set up as fronts to get your business. While some of these plans are good deals, others are expensive and not as good as individual plans.
- As a general rule, purchase one good comprehensive Medicare supplemental policy. There are some exceptions if you have an employer group policy that you can afford but which may have limited benefits. In this case, it may be advisable to have someone knowledgeable go over the options with you.
- Beware of replacing existing coverage. Be suspicious of a suggestion that you give up any policy and buy a replacement. Replacement policies should meet the 1990 standards established by the National Association of Insurance Commissioners which prevent insurers replacing coverage from imposing any additional or new preexisting condition, waiting, elimination, or probationary periods.
- Check your right to renew. Beware of policies that let the company refuse to renew your policy on an individual basis. Pursuant to 1990 standards established by the National Association of Insurance Commissioners, policies must be guaranteed renewable.
- Do not pay cash for insurance. Write a check or money order

payable to the company, not the agent. However, you should not pay for the annual premium until you have received the policy; a deposit should suffice (e.g., one month's premium).

- Keep the agent's and company's name(s), address(es), and telephone number(s). In case of problems you should be able to contact them easily.
- The Medigap insurance market is highly competitive with many products to choose from. Do not let a short-term enrollment period pressure you. Most legitimate policies will not have limited enrollment periods. Some states prohibit special enrollment periods.

HMOs as a Health Care Alternative

Under many health care plans, you have the option of signing up for a Health Maintenance Organization (HMO) or other managed care provider. HMOs are health care delivery systems that provide health care in exchange for a fixed, monthly fee. Under these plans, beneficiaries typically receive all covered hospital and medical insurance benefits through the plan. The cost of this type of plan is known in advance and is generally limited to the fixed monthly premiums and minimal copayments.

At no extra cost, some HMOs provide service beyond what regular health insurance covers. Examples of such services include prescription drugs and hearing aids. However, most HMOs have limits on care that people should be aware of before enrolling.

There are certain advantages to joining an HMO:

- In an HMO, you generally pay a monthly fee, which entitles you to a wide range of medical services. In exchange for the fee, you will not be charged substantial additional costs for your medical care. People who participate in HMOs tend to use their service more frequently and at earlier states of illness.
- The HMO may also absorb any applicable deductibles or coinsurance and provide additional benefits beyond regular services.

- HMOs tend to emphasize preventive health care, an attractive benefit for many people.

There are also certain disadvantages to joining an HMO:

- The main disadvantage is that you may not be able to choose your own doctors and hospital. In general, you must obtain all your health care services through the HMO. In many cases, however, this is not a real problem because many HMOs have excellent doctors and maintain first-rate health care facilities.
- To be eligible for HMO coverage, you may be required to live in the HMO's geographical area for a certain period of time. Therefore, if you travel a great deal, an HMO may not be a viable option for you.
- HMOs do not cover every possible health problem. For example, long-term care, as well as routine dental care, eyeglasses, and hearing aids are generally not covered.

WHAT IS MEDICARE?

Medicare is the federal health insurance program for people age sixty-five or older, certain disabled individuals under age sixty-five who have been collecting Social Security disability benefits for at least twenty-four months, and people of any age who have permanent kidney failure. While Medicare does not cover all medical expenses, it provides some basic protection against the cost of health care.

Do not confuse Medicare with its companion program Medicaid. Medicaid, which is run by state welfare or human service agencies and funded partially by the federal government, is a health insurance program for people with low income and limited assets. A discussion of the Medicaid program appears later in this chapter.

The Health Care Financing Administration is the agency that runs the Medicare program and the Social Security Administration is the agency that handles Medicare enrollment and provides general information. You may qualify for Medicare or Medicaid or both.

There are two basic parts to the Medicare program:

- *Hospital Insurance* (also called "Part A") helps to pay for inpatient hospital care and certain follow-up services. It is financed by part of the payroll (FICA) and self-employment taxes that also pay for Social Security.
- *Medical Insurance* (also called "Part B") helps pay for doctor's services, outpatient hospital care, and certain follow-up services.

These two types of Medicare coverage involve different types of medical costs and different enrollment rules, and they will be discussed separately within this chapter.

ARE YOU ELIGIBLE FOR MEDICARE?

Part A: Hospital Insurance

The majority of people sixty-five or older are eligible for Medicare hospital insurance under Part A based on their own earnings record or that of their spouse. If you meet any of the following requirements, you will be eligible for Medicare Part A hospital insurance at age sixty-five without having to pay monthly premiums:

- You are getting Social Security or Railroad Retirement benefits (Railroad Retirement benefits are equivalent to the Social Security benefits that a railroad employee or beneficiary would have been entitled to receive if the employee's service had been covered under the Social Security system rather than the Railroad Retirement system.)
- You are not getting Social Security or Railroad Retirement benefits, but you have worked long enough to be eligible for them
- You would be entitled to Social Security benefits based on your spouse's earnings record, and your spouse is at least sixty-two (You should be aware that your spouse does not have to apply for benefits in order for you to be eligible based on your spouse's earning record.)

- You have worked long enough for the federal, state, or local government to be insured for Medicare

Prior to age sixty-five, you are eligible for Medicare hospital insurance if you meet either of the following requirements:

- For twenty-four months, you have been getting Social Security disability benefits (In this case you will be automatically enrolled in Medicare.)
- You have worked long enough for the federal, state, or local government and you meet the requirements of the Social Security disability program

Individuals who receive a disability annuity from the Railroad Retirement board should contact their Railroad Retirement office for information on hospital insurance eligibility and any applicable waiting period.

Based on your earnings record, your spouse, divorced spouse, widow or widower, or a dependent parent may qualify for hospital insurance when he or she becomes sixty-five. Further, hospital insurance eligibility may apply to disabled widows and widowers under sixty-five, disabled divorced widows or widowers under sixty-five, and disabled children. Individuals with permanent kidney failure are subject to special rules.

In the event you are ineligible for hospital insurance in the ways outlined, you may be eligible on the basis of government employment in which you paid the Medicare payroll tax. If you are employed by the government and you become disabled before sixty-five, you may be in a position to receive Medicare based on your government work. As a general rule, a twenty-nine-month waiting period will apply before hospital insurance benefits can start. To avoid losing benefit protection under these circumstances, the Social Security Administration suggests you contact them right away.

If you are sixty-five and do not meet the qualifications for premium-free hospital insurance, you can still purchase coverage, in a manner similar to buying private insurance. The basic monthly premium for the Medicare Part A hospital insurance in 1998 is $309 if you have less than thirty quarters of qualifying employment and $170 for more than thirty but less than forty quarters of qualifying employment. You must be a lawfully admitted permanent resident and must live in the United States for five years before you can buy Medicare insurance.

Part B: Medical Insurance

As a general rule, anyone who is sixty-five or older may enroll in Medicare medical insurance and pay the monthly premium ($43.80 in 1998). The same general rule applies to anyone who is under sixty-five and eligible for Part A, hospital insurance. You generally do not need any Social Security or government work credits to obtain coverage under Part B of Medicare. Note that aliens sixty-five or older who are not eligible for Part A, hospital insurance, must be lawfully admitted permanent residents and must live in the United States for five years before they can enroll in Part B, medical insurance.

If you have questions about whether you qualify for Medicare or if you need more information, you may contact the Social Security Administration at 1-800-772-1213 between 7:00 A.M. and 7:00 P.M. every business day. If you receive a Railroad Retirement annuity or Railroad Retirement benefit based on disability, you should contact a Railroad Retirement office.

ENROLLING IN MEDICARE

The enrollment rules for Parts A and B of Medicare are different and you should understand what is required for signing up for Medicare. First, let's review the enrollment procedures for Part A of Medicare.

Enrollment Under Part A

Although an application for hospital insurance under Part A typically must be made, for many people there is automatic enrollment. For example, if you are already receiving Social Security or Railroad Retirement benefits, when you become sixty-five you will be automatically enrolled in Part A, hospital insurance. About two to three months before you turn sixty-five, you will get a package in the mail that will contain your Medicare card, along with information about the Medicare program. Also included will be instructions asking you to decide if you want to pay a monthly premium to sign up for the Part B medical insurance portion of Medicare. If you do not want Part B coverage, you must follow the instructions that come with your Medicare card. If you elect Part B coverage, the premiums for such are automatically deducted from your monthly Social Security check.

If you are planning to retire when you reach sixty-five, you should contact the Social Security Administration about three months before your sixty-fifth birthday. Social Security Administration will sign you up for Medicare at the same time you apply for Social Security benefits. There is no requirement that you must retire in order to get Medicare Part A. However, you will still need to contact Social Security about three months before your sixty-fifth birthday to sign up for Medicare even if you do not retire.

Individuals who are government employees or retirees who are eligible for Medicare because of government work should also contact the Social Security Administration about three months before their sixty-fifth birthday to apply for hospital insurance. A government employee who becomes disabled before age sixty-five may be eligible for Medicare hospital insurance based on his or her government work. As a general rule, there is a twenty-nine-month waiting period before Part A starts. Again, contact your Social Security office to avoid loss of any Medicare protection.

If you are a disabled person under sixty-five, you will be automatically enrolled in hospital insurance and will receive, about three months before you become eligible for Medicare, a Medicare enrollment package containing your Medicare card and information about the program. You become eligible for Part A after you have been entitled to disability benefits for twenty-four months. You will be asked in the package whether you want to pay a monthly premium for Part B medical insurance.

A disabled widow or widower between fifty and sixty-five who has not applied for disability benefits because he or she is already getting another kind of Social Security benefit may still be able to get Medicare Part A hospital insurance. You should contact Social Security as soon as possible so that you will not lose any Medicare protection for which you are eligible. Further, if you or a family member have permanent kidney failure, you should contact your Social Security office to inquire about eligibility and enrollment in Medicare.

If you are an individual who used to get disability insurance benefits and Medicare, but lost them solely because you are working, you can purchase Part A hospital insurance, if you continue to be disabled. And, if you do not meet the regular requirements for entitlement to Medicare, you can purchase coverage by contacting your Social Security office. You should note that you do not have to enroll in Medicare medical insurance unless you choose to do so.

Enrollment Under Part B

If you are enrolled in Part A, you generally may choose to enroll in Part B for a monthly premium. Everyone who enrolls in Part B must pay a monthly premium, as explained below.

Certain people who receive Part A benefits must enroll in Part B. If you are eligible for Medicare benefits because you fall within the following categories, you must enroll in Part B:

- You have chronic kidney failure
- You are not insured under the Social Security or Railroad Retirement system, but wish to receive Medicare benefits (In this case you must pay for both the monthly Part A and Part B premiums)

Most people who have the option of enrolling in Part B choose to do so because it is a very wise buy. The federal government pays approximately 75 percent of the cost of your Part B premiums. It is also extremely unlikely that you could purchase similar private insurance coverage at the current monthly premium cost.

Do not delay enrolling in Part B. If you do not enroll in Part B within the prescribed time, your coverage may be delayed and you may be charged a penalty for late enrollment.

You should contact your Social Security office to apply for Part B medical insurance in any of the following situations:

- You plan to continue working past sixty-five
- You had Part B medical insurance coverage in the past, but eliminated it
- You turned down Part B medical insurance when you became entitled to Part A hospital insurance
- You are sixty-five but are not eligible for hospital insurance
- You are eligible for Medicare based on government work
- You are a disabled widow or widower between fifty and sixty-five and you are not receiving disability benefits
- You live in Puerto Rico or outside the United States

There are two types of enrollment periods for Part B medical insurance: the initial enrollment period and the general enrollment period. It is important for you to know that each period has a specific time frame for enrolling, if you want medical insurance coverage.

The initial enrollment period is seven months. When you are about to become eligible for medical insurance, you have seven months to sign up. This seven-month period begins three months before your sixty-fifth birthday and ends four months after the birthday.

When your coverage begins depends on when you sign up. For example, if you enroll during the first three months, your medical insurance will start with the month you actually become sixty-five. If you sign up during this period, there will be no delay in your coverage. If you sign up during the last four months, your coverage will start one to three months after you sign up. So, you can see why it is so important to avoid any delay.

If you do not sign up during the initial seven-month enrollment period, you cannot sign up until the next general enrollment period. This period runs from January 1 to March 31 of each year. If you enroll during the general enrollment period, your coverage will not start until the following July. In addition, you may be required to pay a monthly premium that is 10 percent higher for each twelve-month period you could have enrolled, but were not enrolled. This 10 percent premium surcharge for late enrollment may not apply if you had employer group health coverage.

MEDICARE TERMINOLOGY

Listed below are definitions for several terms used frequently when discussing the subject of health insurance and health care delivery systems. You will need to know these terms to understand what specific coverage you are obtaining under Medicare.

- *Acute Care:* Care for persons with short-term illness.
- *Approved Charges:* The approved or allowable dollar limit Medicare sets on how much it will pay a provider of medical services for any given treatment or procedure. The fees charged by the medical provider may be above the Medicare limit, up to a predetermined government-imposed ceiling.
- *Benefit Period:* Under Medicare, a benefit period begins the day you enter a hospital and ends when you have been out of the hospital for sixty days in a row.
- *Coinsurance:* A form of cost sharing where an insured individual is required to pay a percentage of covered expenses to a provider.
- *Co-Payment:* Another word for "coinsurance." It may be either a percentage of an approved charge or a flat dollar amount.
- *Custodial Care:* Care that can be given safely and reasonably by a person who is not medically skilled, and which is given mainly to help the patient with daily living.

- *Deductible:* The amount you must pay before the insurance benefits are payable. This payment is a type of cost sharing.
- *Integration:* The way in which a private health insurance plan fits—or "integrates"—with Medicare medical insurance.
- *Long-Term Care:* A broad range of health, social, and supportive services to meet the needs of individuals with some form of disability.
- *Medigap:* Private health insurance which is designed to supplement or fill the gaps in Medicare coverage.
- *Out-of-Pocket Expenses:* Personal payments made for health care not paid for by public or private insurance. The term includes deductible and coinsurance payments, along with payments for products and services that are not covered under insurance plans.
- *Preexisting Condition:* A medical condition that exists at the time you begin coverage under a health insurance plan.
- *Primary Payer:* The health insurance plan that pays first on your hospital and medical bills, as required under legal rules. If the primary payer does not pay all your expenses, the secondary payer may pay the remaining expenses, subject to any deductibles.
- *Reserve Days:* Under Medicare, an extra sixty hospital days that you can use if you have a long illness and have to stay in the hospital for more than ninety days. You are entitled to only sixty reserve days in your lifetime.
- *Secondary Payer:* The health insurance plan that pays after the primary plan has paid hospital and medical expenses.
- *Skilled Nursing Facility:* A medically oriented facility used following recuperation from surgery or in other situations requiring around-the-clock medical care.

What Does Medicare Part A (Hospital Insurance) Cover?

Medicare Part A covers inpatient hospital care, skilled nursing facility care, home health care, and hospice care. Hospitals, skilled nursing facilities, home health care agencies, and hospices are called "providers." If you are hospitalized, your provider will submit its claims directly to Medicare. It is not your responsibility to submit claims for your provider's services.

Your provider will, however, charge you for any part of the Part A deductible you have not met and any coinsurance you owe. It is your responsibility to pay these charges. Note that when your provider sends a Part A claim for payment, you will get a "Notice of Utilization." This will explain the decision that Medicare made on the claim.

Inpatient Hospital Care

Medicare Part A will pay for up to ninety days in any Medicare-participating hospital during each benefit period. For you to be covered, your doctor must prescribe inpatient hospital care for treatment of your injury or illness, and you must require the kind of care that can only be provided by a hospital. For example, in 1998, Part A will pay for all covered services for the first sixty days, except for a deductible of $764. For the sixty-first through the ninetieth days in a hospital, the patient pays $191 per day, while Medicare pays for the remainder of all covered services. If you are out of the hospital for at least sixty days in a row and then return, you will start a new benefit period, and your ninety days of coverage will start all over again.

If you need more than ninety days of inpatient care during any benefit period, you may decide to use some or all of your sixty reserve days. For each reserve day used in 1998, Part A pays for all covered expenses except for $382 per day. Reserve days are not renewable, and once you use a reserve day, you never get it back.

Examples of services and supplies covered by Part A, hospital insurance, include:

- Semiprivate room and meals
- Regular nursing services
- Anesthesia services and operating and recovery room costs
- Intensive care and coronary care
- Drugs, lab tests, and X-rays
- Medical supplies and appliances
- Rehabilitation services, such as physical therapy
- Preparatory services related to kidney transplant surgery

Skilled Nursing Facility Care

In the event you need inpatient skilled nursing or rehabilitation services following a hospital stay, and you meet certain other conditions, Part A helps pay for up to one hundred days in a Medicare-participating skilled nursing facility in each benefit period. To be eligible: (1) Your hospital stay must have been for at least three days, (2) Your inpatient skilled care must, normally, begin within thirty days after leaving the hospital, and (3) This care must be provided by a Medicare-participating skilled nursing facility. Part A pays for all covered services for the first twenty days. For the twenty-first through the hundredth days, it pays for all covered services except for a specified amount per day ($95.50 per day in 1998).

Examples of the services and supplies Medicare pays for when you are in a skilled nursing facility are listed below:

- Semiprivate room and all meals
- Regular nursing services
- Rehabilitation services, such as physical therapy
- Drugs, medical supplies, and medical appliances

You should be aware that Medicare does not pay for custodial care, but for daily skilled care which can only be provided on an inpatient basis.

Home Health Care

In the event you are confined to your home and meet certain other conditions, Part A can pay the full approved cost of home health visits from a Medicare-participating home health agency. No limit is applied to the number of covered visits you can have.

Examples of services Medicare Part A pays for when you need home health care include:

- Part-time skilled nursing care
- Physical therapy
- Speech therapy

Part A also covers part-time services of home health aides, occupational therapy, medical social services, and medical supplies and equipment.

Hospice Care

A facility that provides pain relief and other support services for terminally ill people is known as a hospice. Part A of Medicare can assist in paying for hospice care for terminally ill individuals, if the care is provided by a Medicare-certified hospice and certain other conditions are met.

Generally, Part A can pay for a maximum of two ninety-day periods and one thirty-day period of hospice care. These benefit periods may be used together. Listed below are examples of items that Part A covers when hospice care is needed:

- Doctors' services and nursing services
- Medical appliances and supplies, including outpatient drugs for relief of pain
- Physical and speech therapy
- Home health aide and homemaker services
- Medical social services
- Counseling
- Respite care (inpatient care on a short-term basis in order to give temporary relief to the person who generally assists with home care of the patient)

WHAT DOES MEDICARE PART B (MEDICAL INSURANCE) COVER?

Part B helps pay for doctors' services and other medical services and supplies not covered by Part A hospital insurance. Thus, Part B is helpful if you are sick and do not need to be hospitalized. Prior to Part B paying for covered services, an annual deductible must be met. For example, the 1997 annual deductible was $100. After the deductible is met, Medicare will generally pay 80 percent of the approved amount for covered charges throughout the remainder of the year. It is your responsibility to pay the remaining 20 percent of the charges (i.e., coinsurance) plus the expenses over and beyond the Medicare-approved amount.

Listed below are examples of doctors' services covered by Part B:

- Medical and surgical services, including anesthesia
- Diagnostic tests that are a part of your treatment
- X-rays
- Radiology and pathology services by doctors while you are a hospital inpatient or outpatient
- Treatment of mental illness (payments for outpatient treatment are limited to 50 percent of approved charge instead of 80 percent)
- Services of your doctor's office nurse
- Drugs that cannot be self-administered, blood transfusions, and other medical supplies

Examples of other services covered by Part B include:

- Outpatient hospital services you receive for diagnosis and treatment of an illness, including care in an emergency room or outpatient clinic of a hospital
- An unlimited number of home health visits if you do not have hospital insurance and if certain conditions are met
- Ambulance transportation
- Home dialysis equipment and support services
- Outpatient physical therapy and speech pathology services
- Radiation treatments

Medicare determines what is a reasonable charge for each service you receive. If the charges for your services are more than the Medicare-approved amount, you generally will owe the Medicare coinsurance (20 percent of the Medicare-approved amount), plus any charges above the Medicare-approved amount.

If your doctor accepts "assignment," you pay only the coinsurance amount. Thus, by choosing a doctor that accepts assignment, you could save many dollars. "Assignment" is a method by which Medicare pays your doctor. If your doctor "accepts assignment," he or she agrees to accept the "Medicare-approved" charge as total payment for the services that he or she has provided. Doctors who accept assignment are said to be "Medicare-participating."

To find out if your doctor accepts assignment, you can do one of the following:

- Call the Medicare carrier in your state and ask for a free copy of the Medicare-Participating Physician/Supplier Directory for your area. Medicare "carriers," also called "intermediaries," are health insurance organizations that are under contract with Medicare to process Medicare claims.
- Ask your doctor/supplier if he or she accepts assignment. Often Medicare-participating doctors/suppliers display emblems or certificates which show that they accept assignment on all Medicare claims.

After your doctor/supplier sends in a Part B claim, Medicare will send you a notice called an "Explanation of Medicare Benefits." This form will show you what Medicare paid for and why. For example, if you received services from a doctor, this notice should contain all of the following information:

- Whether your doctor took assignment on your claim
- The date and type of services that you received
- The amount billed and the amount approved
- The amount Medicare paid

- Whether you have met your annual deductible
- The amount for which you are responsible

Be sure that you review this form carefully and save it for your records. If you suspect a mistake, call or write the carrier that handled your claim.

If you believe that payment has been incorrectly denied, you have the right to ask the carrier to review the decision. Often, asking for a review is worth the effort. A majority of reviews are resolved in favor of the beneficiary. If you are unable to resolve your dispute with the carrier, you can take legal action before an administrative law judge or in court.

WHAT DOES MEDICARE EXCLUDE?

The Medicare program is designed to provide basic health care coverage for the elderly and the disabled, but it does not pay all your medical expenses. Listed below are examples of the services and supplies not covered by Medicare:

- Custodial care
- Most nursing-home care
- Care you get outside the United States (Canada and Mexico may be exceptions if inpatient care is given in a Medicare-certified hospital)
- Routine checkups and the tests directly related to these checkups (please note: some mammograms and Pap smears are covered)
- Routine dental care and dentures
- Most immunization shots
- Prescription drugs
- Routine foot care
- Medical tests for, and the cost of, eyeglasses or hearing aids
- Personal comfort items, such as a telephone or television

What Happens If You Have Other Health Insurance?

If you have other health insurance when you become eligible for Medicare, you need to decide whether it is worth the monthly premium cost to you to sign up for Part B, medical insurance. Here are some tips to help your decision-making process:

- Find out how your private health insurance plan "integrates" with Part B
- Determine how you and your family members will be impacted with or without Part B coverage
- Keep in mind that most private plans, similar to Medicare, do not cover all health services
- Remember that most nursing-home care is not covered by private health insurance policies or Medicare
- Protect yourself and be sure not to cancel any health insurance you now have until your Medicare coverage actually begins

You should be aware of the following special rules, if you have health insurance from an employer group health plan:

- You can wait to enroll in Medicare medical insurance during a seven-month "special enrollment period," if you work past sixty-five or are sixty-five or older and the spouse of a worker of any age. The enrollment period begins with the month the group health coverage ends or the month employment ends, whichever comes first. If you meet certain requirements, you will not have to pay monthly premiums that are 10 percent higher for late enrollment in Medicare.
- In a group health plan that covers at least one employer with twenty or more employees, the group health plan is required by law to offer workers who are sixty-five or older the same health benefits that are provided to younger employees. Further, the group health plan must also offer the spouses who are sixty-five or older (regardless of the age of the worker) the same health benefits given younger spouses. If you or your

spouse continue to belong to your employer's group health plan, Medicare will be the secondary payer and the employer plan will be the primary payer. If you reject your employer's plan, Medicare will be the primary health insurance payer. You should be aware that the employer is not allowed to offer you Medicare supplemental coverage if you reject its health plan.

- If you are under sixty-five, disabled, and have health coverage under your employer's health plan or a family member's employer health plan, Medicare will be the secondary payer. The employer plan must be a "large group health plan," that is, a plan that covers employees of at least one employer who has one hundred or more employees. In this situation, you will have a special enrollment period and will not be subject to the 10 percent premium surcharge.
- If you are under sixty-five, entitled to Medicare because of permanent kidney failure, and have employer group health coverage, Medicare will be the secondary payer for an initial twelve-month period. When that period ends, Medicare will be your primary payer.

HEALTH MAINTENANCE ORGANIZATIONS AND MEDICARE

As a general rule, Medicare beneficiaries have options with respect to how and where they receive their Medicare-covered services. Many choose a particular doctor or hospital approved under Medicare. Under this arrangement, the bill is sent to Medicare after the service is provided. You (or your Medigap plan) are responsible for any amounts that Medicare does not cover. However, you also have the option of signing up for a managed care provider such as an HMO.

As explained earlier, HMOs are health care delivery systems that provide health care in exchange for a monthly, fixed fee. Under these plans, Medicare beneficiaries receive all Medicare-covered hospital and medical insurance benefits through the plan. Call or visit a Social Security office if you want to find out how to contact an HMO in your area for more information.

MEDICAID

The Medicaid program was enacted in 1965 as Medicare's companion program. It is a joint federal-state medical assistance program that is operated by the states with partial federal funding. The Medicaid program supplements Medicare by providing comprehensive health care benefits for individuals ages sixty-five and older and disabled individuals who have very low incomes and assets. Individuals eligible for Medicaid include the following:

- Persons receiving Aid to Families with Dependent Children (AFDC) benefits
- Persons receiving Supplemental Security Income (SSI) benefits
- Persons with low income (defined by each state) who meet their individual state's eligibility requirements
- Low-income pregnant women and children under the age of six

The Medicaid program was originally thought of as a vehicle for providing health care for the poor, without regard to age. Today Medicaid is a major payer of long-term care, especially inpatient skilled nursing-home care. Often, individuals with medical expenses have been forced to "spend down" their income and assets to the pre-set level that triggers or initiates Medicaid eligibility. On this point, you should note that there are "spousal impoverishment" rules. The rules are designed to assist beneficiaries in avoiding the use of their entire life savings before qualifying for Medicaid nursing-home coverage.

By law, every state Medicaid program is required to pay for medical expenses generally included under Medicare Part A and Part B, including the following:

- Inpatient hospital services
- Outpatient hospital services

- Skilled nursing facility care
- Physicians fees
- Laboratory tests
- Home health care services

Some states may choose to provide additional Medicaid coverage for benefits such as dental care and prescription drugs.

In the event you are eligible for Medicaid, the need for Medigap insurance should be reevaluated. It is likely that the benefits you purchase under Medigap insurance would duplicate your benefits under Medicaid. Further, your Medigap premiums could be financially prohibitive.

HEALTH CARE FROM NURSING HOMES

The term "nursing home" means different things to different people. For some, any permanent place of residence for older people, other than their own home, is considered to be a nursing home. For others, it is a place where older people can receive continuing medical care, and, for still others, it is a warehouse for unwanted older persons.

We will use the term "nursing home" to mean a housing arrangement that provides a complete spectrum of health, social, and supportive services to older persons in need of assistance on a long-term or rehabilitative care basis. Although nursing homes primarily serve an older population, they also provide care to any person, regardless of age, who is in need of long-term or rehabilitative services unavailable through home care or hospitals.

Nursing homes are generally divided into three major categories: (1) skilled-care nursing homes, (2) intermediate-care nursing homes, and (3) custodial- or residential-care nursing homes. The different types of nursing homes, most of which are privately owned and operated, reflect the functions provided by the facilities and the needs of the residents. Both the federal and state governments have strict rules (though less strict for custodial-care nursing homes) which regulate how the homes are staffed and managed. Federal standards must be met for Medicare and Medicaid reimbursement and each home must be licensed by the state in which it operates. A brief description of each type follows.

- *Skilled-Care Nursing Homes:* These facilities are for patients who require intensive, around-the-clock supervision and complex medical care by a registered nurse, under the direction of a physician.
- *Intermediate-Care Nursing Homes:* These nursing homes are for patients who benefit from around-the-clock assistance because of disabilities, but who can still perform many daily life activities alone, such as dressing and eating. This type of facility provides supportive care with low level of medical care.
- *Custodial- or Residential-Care Nursing Homes:* These facilities, also referred to as board-and-care or personal-care homes, are for patients who require supervision with respect to daily life activities. As a general rule, the patients do not require medical care.

When a long-term illness strikes, most retirees find that the long-term care that they need, such as nursing-home care, is not adequately covered by Medicare, other public programs, or their private insurance. Because nursing-home care is often needed over an extended period of time, nursing-home costs are one of the greatest threats to the financial security of retirees. Remember that Medicare only covers one hundred days in a skilled nursing facility immediately following a hospital stay. Many private long-term care insurance policies have limitations and exclusions which severely restrict coverage for nursing-home care. This means that Medicaid has become the primary source of funding for nursing-home care for most senior citizens.

The eligibility requirements for Medicaid vary from state to state, but typically require that your income and assets be lower than the levels established by the state in which you live. You should contact the appropriate agency on aging, public welfare, or social services which handles Medicaid applications in your state for specific eligibility requirements.

Many states use the eligibility rules for Supplemental Security Income (SSI) under Social Security in determining qualifications for Medicaid. These eligibility rules for SSI are discussed further in chapter 9. The rules for eligibility typically require that your income be below established poverty guidelines and that your cash and liquid assets not exceed prescribed amounts. However, the SSI rules permit you to keep other assets such as your family home, a certain amount of household goods, automobiles and other vehicles, certain life insurance, and funds for burial expenses, while still being eligible for Medicaid, .

The eligibility rules place some restrictions on the transfer of assets to become eligible for Medicaid. Assets transferred to or held in trust for a Medicaid applicant will be counted as available resources in determining eligibility. After July 1, 1988, an institutionalized applicant for Medicaid can be denied eligibility if he or she transferred assets at less than fair market value within thirty months of applying for Medicaid. This period of ineligibility generally lasts until the time required to "spend-down" the uncompensated value of the transferred assets on medical care, but cannot exceed thirty months. Transfer of a home is excluded from these rules if the transfer is to a spouse, dependent or disabled child, or to a sibling or nondependent son or daughter under certain conditions.

If your income or assets exceed the eligibility guidelines for Medicaid, you will be notified when you apply that you are over-income. A "spend-down" amount will be specified which you must spend toward allowable expenses before you are eligible for Medicaid benefits. Chapter 7 provides a discussion on handling your assets to maximize benefits such as nursing-home care.

Since the financing of nursing-home care is extremely expensive, be sure to read any admission documents and contracts very carefully. The advice of an attorney knowledgeable in this area is suggested, given the complexity of the rules and other issues relating to nursing-home care. You should seek the attorney's advice before you or someone in your care enters the home. Without a comprehensive review, you or a relative may be held personally liable for expenses.

Under federal law, nursing home residents have rights that must be met by every nursing home participating in Medicare or Medicaid. Such rights include receiving information about the following:

- Their residential rights
- The services offered by the nursing home and the fees for those services
- Plans for their medical care and treatment

Additionally, patients have the right to make choices for themselves about physicians, activities in which they engage, and to voice grievances; to have privacy in social, religious, medical, and communication arenas; and to be free from abuse and restraint. Patients must be treated with dignity and respect.

When reviewing a nursing-home agreement, you should be on the look out for the following:

- Admission fees—check current status of state and federal law regarding the permissibility of such fees
- Differential rates and rooms for private-pay residents
- Medicare coverage—check who covers costs in absence of Medicare eligibility
- Payment-in-advance clauses
- Personal care expenses
- Application fees

For more information on this subject, request the American Association of Retired Persons' (AARP) publication, *Nursing Home Life: A Guide for Residents and Families.* AARP's address appears in the Appendix.

CHAPTER 6

Planning for Disability

All of us are likely to have difficult times in our lives when we will need the help and trust of others. Finding someone who will care for you and manage your affairs if you become incapacitated or disabled is a very important task for you to accomplish. You can plan ahead for many of these situations by making a durable power of attorney, living will, or medical directive explicitly stating your choices.

Appointing Someone to Manage Your Affairs

A power of attorney is basically a written document whereby you authorize someone else to act on your behalf. If you make a power of attorney, you are commonly referred to as the principal. The person to whom you have given the power of attorney to act on your behalf is referred to as your agent.

A power of attorney can be useful to you in a variety of situations. It can be useful if you are undergoing an operation or going away for an extended period of time. For almost anything that you can do for yourself, you can give a power of attorney to someone to act on your behalf. This includes the power to contract, buy and sell property, cash checks, make deposits and withdrawals, settle claims, file lawsuits, and almost anything else. Your power of attorney serves as evidence to others that you have appointed someone to act on your behalf. It can also serve as an agreement between you and your agent regarding the business to be transacted under your power of attorney.

Although a general power of attorney normally terminates when you become incapacitated, you can make a durable power of attorney which will remain valid even if you later lose the capacity to contract and appoint an agent. Your durable power of attorney typically must be in writing, signed by you, and it must contain language which shows that you intend your power of attorney to remain in effect even if you are disabled or incapacitated.

DURABLE POWER OF ATTORNEY

A durable power of attorney is essential if you plan to appoint someone to make decisions for you in the event that you are incapacitated. Remember, if you are seriously ill, unconscious, or lacking mental capacity, you will not be able to make decisions concerning your medical treatment and personal or business affairs. Unless you designate someone to act on your behalf by durable power of attorney or otherwise, a guardian may have to be appointed by the courts to make decisions for you. Appointment of a guardian is not only a lengthy and costly legal process, but it could result in the appointment of someone that you might not want to make choices for you.

Your power of attorney can be general to cover broad areas regarding your affairs, or it can be limited to specific acts or responsibilities. You do not give up control over your affairs when you execute a power of attorney, rather you maintain control by simply designating a person who has the authority to act for you under certain circumstances. For example, you can sign a "health-care power of attorney" or "medical proxy" wherein you authorize someone to specifically make health care decisions for you in the event that you are unable to speak for yourself. You can usually revoke your power of attorney at any time.

LIVING WILLS AND MEDICAL DIRECTIVES

In addition to appointing someone to make health care decisions for you, you can express your desire to refuse life-prolonging medical treatment in the event of terminal illness or injury. Your right to refuse treatment when you are unable to make decisions and have no chance for recovery can be carried out by making a "living will" (also referred to as a "medical directive"). A "living will" is not a will at all, but instructions to family members or doctors regarding the continuation or termination of medical life-support systems. You can execute a living will if you wish to avoid life-support systems that only prolong the dying process.

Many states, including Alabama, Alaska, Arizona, Arkansas, California, Colorado, Connecticut, Delaware, Florida, Georgia, Hawaii, Idaho, Illinois, Indiana, Iowa, Kansas, Louisiana, Maine, Maryland, Mississippi, Missouri, Montana, Nevada, New Hampshire, New Mexico, North Carolina, Oklahoma, Oregon, South Carolina, Tennessee, Texas, Utah, Vermont, Virginia, Washington, West Virginia, Wisconsin, and Wyoming, as well as the District of Columbia have adopted "living will," "death-with-dignity," or "right-to-die" laws which recognize the rights of terminally ill patients to stop life support. These laws are intended to protect doctors, hospitals, and others from civil and criminal liability, and to honor the wishes of patients who are dying from a terminal condition.

A typical death-with-dignity law provides that a terminally ill patient can request by conscious directive or living will that life-sustaining medical treatment be withheld or withdrawn. The hospital, staff, and family will be free from liability if such a request is honored. The laws also protect any insurance that the terminal patient may have, by providing that honoring a living will does not constitute suicide.

The requirements for making a living will are governed by the laws of your particular state. Generally, it is required that your living will be signed and dated by you when you are in a stable mental and physical condition. Typically, it must be witnessed by two or more people who are not your relatives, doctor or doctor's employees, beneficiaries, or creditors. You and your witnesses usually must be at least eighteen years of age. You should have the signatures notarized so that your living will is self-proving.

The living will document itself basically provides that if the situation should arise in which there is no reasonable expectation of recovery from terminal physical or mental disability, you request that you be allowed to die naturally, and not be kept alive by artificial means or extraordinary measures. If you make a living will, be sure to give copies to your doctor and family so that they will know your wishes. If you change doctors, be sure your new doctor gets a copy. Update and re-sign it periodically to show that it is still current.

Before your living will is honored, usually a determination of terminal illness or condition must be made by your attending physician and at least one other doctor. Some doctors or hospitals may be reluctant to honor your living will and terminate life-support system, unless specifically requested by some authorized person at that time. For this reason, you should make a durable health-care power of attorney or medical proxy a part of your living will, whereby you appoint someone to make medical decisions for you and carry out the directives of your living will.

Your choice of agent is very important in making a power of attorney, especially a health-care power of attorney or medical proxy. You should appoint someone you trust and who will act in your best interest. Remember, the person you appoint will have great power over your affairs and personal care.

BUYING PRIVATE HEALTH AND DISABILITY INSURANCE

In planning for disability, you also need to prepare for the financial burden of long-term illness and health care. Remember, Medicare pays for less than half of an older person's annual health care bills and less than 2 percent of nursing home costs. Medicaid covers only about 40 percent of nursing home expenses for those who meet low-income requirements. Yet, over the past decade, medical costs and the gaps in Medicare coverage have grown beyond anticipation. Insurance companies are now offering a variety of private health, long-term care, and disability insurance plans. You should review your needs and consider obtaining health and disability insurance if necessary.

Nearly three quarters of older Americans purchase Medicare supplemental insurance (Medigap) to fill gaps in their coverage. These Medigap policies, however, typically have limitations; insuring you against only that portion of your medical costs that are not covered by Medicare. Oftentimes the Medigap policies cover services only after Medicare pays first. Therefore, if payment for a service is denied by Medicare, your Medigap insurance also may not pay.

Selecting a proper Medigap insurance plan can be difficult. Too often, many seniors buy the wrong insurance and end up paying too much and getting overlapping or inadequate protection. There is a lot of misunderstanding about whether Medigap insurance covers nursing-home care. Medigap insurance generally does not cover the care of senior citizens who can no longer care for themselves. Likewise, none of the costs for custodial care are covered by Medicare.

Do not let your fear of illness or disability push you to buy supplemental health insurance that is not right for you. Before you buy a Medigap policy, determine what you need in supplemental health insurance and examine the Medigap policy providing this coverage. Compare the premium, waiting periods, preexisting condition clauses, exclusions, and benefits of several insurance plans and purchase the one that is most cost effective and comprehensive for you. Go over the fine print with an attorney or some other able person you trust. Be certain that you fully understand the policy's coverage and limitations before you buy insurance.

Watch out for insurance policies that can cancel your coverage for any reason. Also be aware of policies that exclude coverage for a preexisting condition.

CHAPTER 7

Handling Real Estate and Other Assets for Maximum Benefits

THERE IS MORE AND MORE CONCERN BY RETIREES AND THEIR families about the need to preserve family assets from catastrophic health care costs, unnecessary taxes, creditors, estate expenses, and oppressive lawsuits. Additionally, Medicaid eligibility, nursing-home care, and recovery of health-care cost by the government are critical issues of concern. It is easy for retirees to underestimate the importance of these matters until they hit.

Remember that basic nursing-home care typically costs over $50,000 a year, and the average stay in a nursing home is thirty months. It is estimated that over half of the people receiving nursing-home care go broke trying to pay for it. Medicaid eligibility, personal assets, and long-term care insurance are the main factors to consider when planning for nursing-home care.

In determining Medicaid eligibility, the state looks at the assets and the monthly income of the applicant. As discussed in chapter 5, certain assets are not counted against the applicant in determining Medicaid eligibility, such as primary residence; $2,000 in cash, one vehicle, household goods, personal effects and jewelry, prepaid irrevocable burial plan, $1,500 in a burial fund account or burial plots, $1,500 cash-value in life insurance, and unlimited term life insurance. In addition, the spouse usually gets to keep one-half of the total nonexempt assets and is also allowed an income allowance for monthly living; which may allow some assets and income shifting from the applicant to the spouse.

Planning for long-term care may involve shifting or turning non-exempt assets into exempt assets. For example, you can purchase, improve, or pay off a loan on a residence, or buy prepaid funeral and burial plots, long-term care insurance, an annuity, household goods, and personal effects.

Keep in mind that real estate, particularly your home, plays a special role in how you manage your assets for maximum benefit. The home is one of the major assets of most retirees and must be a key component in any estate, financial, tax, or retirement planning.

Managing Your Home Asset

To effectively manage your home or personal residence as an asset, you must understand the general rules affecting the most common transactions which retirees engage in that can impact their homes. This includes the tax laws, estate laws, Medicaid eligibility rules, financing requirements, as well as personal liability and insurance factors. You may need to work with a legal, tax, or financial specialist to assure that the appropriate planning is implemented.

The major tax planning issues to be addressed are when and how to sell, buy, or finance a personal residence so as to result in the least amount of tax consequences. These issues include:

- The one-time $125,000 exclusion of gain when a home owner who is at least fifty-five years old sells his principal residence
- The roll-over of gain on the sale of an old principal residence into the purchase of a new principal residence
- The new universal exemption of up to $500,000 for gain on sale of a residence
- The deductibility of certain moving expenses associated with relocating to a new residence where the move is work-related

- The deductible expenses related to financing a home
- The technique of reverse financing to provide for retirement income

In many cases, retirees find that the sale of their home is necessary for retirement. This typically happens because the retiree wants to downscale his housing facilities, free-up some money, or retire to another location. In these situations, the sale of the home might result in a large capital gain which could be taxable if appropriate steps are not taken.

For many years, the capital gains from the sale of a principal residence received special treatment under the federal tax laws. Homeowners who were age fifty-five or older were able to permanently exclude from taxable income up to $125,000 of gain from the sale of their home by making a special once-in-a-lifetime election. Also, a homeowner of any age could defer all or part of the gain from the sale of his home by buying a qualifying replacement home within two years before or after the sale. The above-mentioned tax treatment is still available for home sales prior to May 7, 1997.

However, for sales of principal residences on or after May 7, 1997, the new tax law essentially does away with the previous $125,000 exclusion and the deferral of gain toward a replacement, and replaces them with a new universal exclusion. The new exclusion should benefit most homeowners and provides for an exclusion of gain of up to $500,000 for qualifying homeowners. Under the new tax law, an individual can exclude up to $250,000 in gain from the sale or other disposition of his or her primary residence. A qualifying married couple filing a joint tax return can exclude as much as $500,000 of gain.

Keep in mind also that the home typically represents an asset of considerable value which is included in the owner's estate upon his death. Working with a good legal, financial, or tax advisor to develop an adequate estate plan, you can avoid or defer estate taxes. Your estate planning should take advantage of the unified tax credit which exempts $625,000 ($1,250,000 if assets are properly transferred to a spouse) of assets from estate taxes.

It might be beneficial in some situations for a retiree to transfer ownership of his home to his children or other heirs to remove the value of the home from his estate. This can be done by giving away interests in the home by a deed, irrevocable trust, or other manner. When making gifts, be sure to take advantage of the gift tax exclusion of $10,000 per year for each recipient. Various irrevocable trust arrangements such as the "qualified personal residence trust" or "family partnership trust" can be used to transfer ownership of your home to avoid taxes, creditors, and lawsuits. With the qualified personal residence trust, you transfer the entire ownership of your home to a trust while retaining the right to live in the home for a period of time. At the end of the time period, the ownership of the home would then be transferred to the beneficiaries of the trust.

Placing your home or other assets in an irrevocable trust has several tax advantages. An irrevocable trust is trust arrangement created during the life of the grantor wherein the grantor does not retain the right to revoke or amend the trust. Generally the assets in an irrevocable trust are not included in the taxable estate of the grantor. Additionally, the irrevocable trust may be taxed on trust income as a separate entity from the grantor, which could lead to tax savings for taxpayers who are in the high tax brackets. An irrevocable trust can also shield assets from creditors except to the extent the grantor or beneficiaries receive income or principal from the trust. Further, an irrevocable trust may be used to protect the assets of the grantor, grantor's spouse, and children from health care costs while enabling them to qualify for Medicaid and other government benefits.

A common housing transaction for many retirees is to sell their home and relocate to Florida, the Carolinas, a retirement village, or other popular retirement spots where the retiree or his or her spouse will take on some type of employment at the new location (e.g., working full- or part-time, or operating a consulting or other business). The tax deduction for moving expenses can be significant, and tax and retirement planning should take advantage of this moving expense deduction where applicable.

In many cases retirees will want to refinance their homes to raise money for retirement expenditures, medical care, vacations, or other important reasons. While interest on a mortgage to buy a home is deductible for tax purposes, other loans or mortgages must qualify as home equity financing for the interest to be tax deductible. Home equity financing is permitted up to $100,000, in addition to any home acquisition mortgage, and must be secured by a lien on the home. However, the home equity loan can be used for any purpose.

Reverse mortgages may be another refinancing option for the retired homeowner. Many retirees will own their homes free and clear of any mortgages, and a reverse mortgage can be used to provide money to supplement fixed incomes or to take care of any retirement or other matters. With a reverse mortgage, the homeowner is usually paid a lump sum or monthly installments over a period of time, or has access to a line of credit. The reverse mortgage loan is typically due and payable when you stop living in your home or title is transferred to someone else.

Reverse mortgages have gained in popularity since Fannie Mae introduced its reverse mortgage program in 1995. To qualify for a reverse mortgage under the Fannie Mae program, you must be at least sixty-two years old and must occupy the home as your principal residence during the term of the mortgage. As long as you abide by the terms of the mortgage agreement, you cannot be forced to sell or vacate your home. However, the reverse mortgage loan cannot exceed the equity in your home. If the reverse mortgage is structured as a loan there should be no tax consequences because of the payments received from the lender. Thus, a reverse mortgage can provide a retiree with the opportunity to continue living at home as desired and supplement retirement income through the payments received under the reverse mortgage.

However, a reverse mortgage may not be appropriate for

everyone. There are origination fees, closing costs, mortgage insurance, and/or servicing fees which are assessed up front. Although you can usually finance these items as part of your loan, you will need to remain in your home for a substantial period of time to benefit from a reverse mortgage. If you plan to move in a few years or if you wish to pass the equity in your home to your heirs, then the reverse mortgage is probably not appropriate for you.

Protecting Assets from Nursing Home Costs

The catastrophic cost of nursing-home care can wipe out your assets unless you have done adequate planning. The costs of one year in a nursing home can be $50,000 or more, and in most cases these costs are paid for by the patient or his or her family. Medicaid will cover long-term care in a nursing home but to qualify you must be impoverished or become impoverished. Medicaid eligibility rules essentially make it all but impossible to receive nursing-home care without spending down all of your assets. In most cases, you'll be required to turn over most of your life savings to the nursing home before Medicaid will pay any costs.

Although Medicaid rules are fairly complex, if you know them and arrange your finances accordingly, you might be able to protect your assets and still qualify for nursing-home assistance.

There is nothing wrong about arranging your financial affairs in a way to maximize your benefits as allowed under the law. While the law basically provides that you can't transfer assets to your children or others in anticipation of going into a nursing home, there are several perfectly legal ways to protect your assets. There are a variety of strategies to obtain or accelerate Medicaid eligibility. In order to determine what strategy should be used, it is first necessary to review health and financial data and goals. Several strategies are typically used in combination.

In each state, a Medicaid recipient may have a set limit in countable assets and qualify for Medicaid. One way to achieve this limit is to "spend down" by paying off debts or making payments for legal, medical, or other services.

A useful strategy in Medicaid planning is to review the family assets and determine which, if any, can be converted to non-countable assets while, at the same time, furthering family goals. Typical strategies include buying household or personal goods, making home improvements, buying a new home or car, prepaying funeral expenses, withdrawing cash value from life insurance, and purchasing an annuity. All of these take advantage of Medicaid rules which allow you to shelter noncountable assets.

There are also strategies for transferring assets to others which can provide benefits under the Medicaid eligibility rules. Typically, assets transferred to a spouse are exempt and not countable in determining Medicaid eligibility. Transferring the home to a child, sibling, or caregiver under certain circumstances is also permitted under Medicaid.

As the Medicaid rules can be complex, it is important that you seek advice from a good legal specialist in the Medicaid area.

CHAPTER 8

PREPARING A WILL AND LIVING TRUST

IF YOU HAVE NOT MADE A WILL AT THIS POINT IN YOUR LIFE, THERE are several good reasons why you should prepare one. Your will expresses your specific wishes as to how you want your property distributed and it eliminates speculation and confusion about how your estate will be given away. Also, it states who you want to handle your estate. Equally important, your will provides a good inventory of your property and assets. Without this, it may be difficult for someone to identify and locate any real estate, bank accounts, safe deposit boxes, securities, or other personal property you may have in various places. Preparing your will is also good because it causes you to seriously consider the full extent of your property, family, and friends, and to plan your estate accordingly.

In earlier times a will was the most common means of handling the disposition of a person's estate. Today, however, if you want to create an estate plan, you have a variety of will substitutes and alternatives to the traditional will. For example, you can hold property in joint tenancy with right of survivorship, whereby the property will automatically pass to the surviving co-owner upon your death. You can also put property into a living trust to have it transferred directly to named beneficiaries without having to go through probate. Even if you use one of the alternative estate planning methods, you should still prepare a will to cover any residual property and as a backup in case the joint tenancy, living trust, or other alternative fails.

Gathering Information to Prepare Your Will

Before making your will, you should prepare a list of all of your real and personal property. This list should be complete with all your real estate, bank accounts, safe deposit boxes, stocks and bonds, automobiles, furniture, jewelry, artwork, and all other assets. It is also good to list any insurance policies you may have, even though insurance proceeds will generally be paid directly to the beneficiary named in the policy. You should also prepare a list of your children, spouse, other family members, friends, charities, and others whom you would like to make beneficiaries in your will.

Next, you should prepare a distribution plan which shows how you want your property distributed among your family, friends, and others. Identify someone that you would like to name as executor (male) or executrix (female) to carry out your wishes and the distribution of your estate. You should also identify an alternate person in the event that the first executor or executrix is unable to serve.

With all the information you have just gathered, you can now prepare your will. You can prepare a simple will yourself using a standard will form. For a complex will an attorney may be required.

Requirements for Making a Valid Will

A will is a legal document that is prepared with certain formalities and under which you direct what will happen to your property after your death. Your will is effective only upon your death and it can be modified or revoked by you at any time during your life. If you should die without leaving a will, your property will be distributed according to state law and will generally go to your spouse and children or other next of kin.

The formal requirements for making a valid will depend on your state law. However, most of the states have four general requirements for the formation of a valid will. First, there must be the necessary intent to make a will. This means that you must intend for the document and the words contained therein to operate as your will upon your death. Secondly, you must be of legal age and have the legal capacity to make a will. This means that you must have actual knowledge of the act that you are performing. You must also have an understanding of your property and your relationship to others at the time of making your will. Third, your will must be made free of fraud, duress, undue influence, and mistake. Fourth, your will must be executed in accordance with the formal requirements of your state law. This generally requires that your will be signed by you and by two disinterested witnesses in the presence of each other. Some states may require that the will be witnessed by three people. Therefore, it is recommended that you have at least three people sign your will as witnesses.

You must have the intent to make a will for your will to be valid. This is a question of fact which is determined from the circumstances surrounding the making of your will. Where your will is a sham or was executed as a joke, the requirement testamentary intent is lacking and your will is invalid. If you prepare a document or agreement which shows an intent to make a will in the future, this document or agreement is not a valid will. For your will to be valid, it must show your present intent to make a will.

For the required testamentary capacity to make a will, you must be of legal age and sound mental capacity. The legal age in most states is eighteen years. The sound mental capacity requires that you be able to understand all of the following:

1. The relationship between you and the natural objects of your generosity (i.e., spouse, children, and other family members)

2. The nature and extent of your property
3. That you are executing your will

The required mental capacity must exist at the time that you make your will. If you should later lose the required mental capacity, this does not affect the validity of an earlier will executed when you did have the required mental capacity.

Your capacity to make a will can be influenced by alcohol, drugs, medications, illness, and mental disease. To help avoid questions about your capacity to make a will, your will should contain an introductory clause declaring that you are of sound mind and body, have full testamentary intent and capacity, and voluntarily execute that document as your last will and testament. Your will should also include a witness attestation clause in which the witnesses declare that you are of sound mind and body and signed of your free will.

Signing and Witnessing Your Will

The valid execution of your will requires that it be signed by you. Your signature generally must appear at the end of the will. However, it is recommended that you sign at the end of each page to prevent fraud and substitution of pages. You should use your regular and complete signature, although any name or make used by you and intended as your signature is generally acceptable. You should sign your will in the presence of the witnesses who will be attesting to it. If you are unable to sign your will, generally you can have another person sign for you. This must be done in your presence and in the presence of the witnesses and be at your specific direction.

It is required that your will be witnessed by two or three people, depending on state law. This usually requires that the witnesses observe your signing and also sign the will themselves in your presence and the presence of each other. Who may be a witness to your will is also governed by your state law. Generally, any competent person who is of legal age can be a witness. Some states require that to act as a witness, the person cannot be a beneficiary or lose gifts under the will. Therefore, it is recommended that your will be witnessed by disinterested witnesses who will not be beneficiaries under your will.

Your will should contain a witness attestation clause which declares that the will was signed and published in their presence and that you were of sound mind and body and acting from your free will at that time. This witness attestation clause may be useful in preventing challenges to your will that might be based on arguments that you lacked testamentary intent and capacity. Your witnesses should include their addresses along with their signatures so they will be easier to find, if necessary.

Your will can be "self-proving" if your signature and those of your witnesses are notarized. If your will is "self-proving," the signatures are presumed to be valid and authentic. This would make it difficult for someone to challenge your will by claiming that the signatures are not genuine. For this reason, it is recommended that you and your witnesses sign the will before a notary and have it notarized.

What Should Your Will Provide?

Generally, there are no required provisions for inclusion in a will. Each person's will is unique in that it contains instructions on how he or she would like to have his or her property given away. Make sure that your will expresses your particular wishes and desires.

Your will should contain a declaration that you are of sound mind and body and free will, that you have full testamentary intent and capacity, and that you voluntarily make your will. Also include your current domicile.

Your will should also include a clause expressly revoking any previous wills or codicils executed by you. A "codicil" is an amendment to a will which does not revoke it, but merely modifies it. Your new will should always be intended to supersede any earlier wills or codicils and a revocation clause makes these intentions clear.

An executor or executrix should be appointed under your will to handle your estate. Most people name their spouse, attorney, or a close friend, and provide that no bond be required to carry out his or her duties under the will. You should direct your executor or executrix to pay all of your just debts and other expenses of the administration of your estate. These debts and expenses are usually paid directly from the assets of your estate before any distribution is made to your beneficiaries.

Your will should contain provisions for gifts to your beneficiaries. In the simplest form these can be gifts of specific property to named individuals. You may also make gifts to members of a class, such as your children, brothers or sisters, and the like. In order to be valid, any gift must be ascertainable within twenty-one years after the life of a specific person named in the will. For complicated will and trust provisions you should consult an attorney.

In many states, your surviving spouse may be entitled to a certain minimum portion (usually from one-quarter to one-half) of your estate regardless of what your will provides. Thus, you may need to indicate in your will whether any bequest or devise to your spouse is in lieu of, or in addition to, any minimum portion mandated by state law. Likewise, some states provide that a child who is not mentioned or provided for in your will may be entitled to a share of your estate. Similar provisions may apply to children born after execution of your will. For these reasons, your state law should be checked for specific provisions of testamentary gifts to children. It is recommended that all your children be acknowledged and mentioned in your will, even if you do not leave them anything or only leave a small token gift.

Be sure to include a residuary clause in your will wherein you give the remainder of your estate. This provision is important in case you have omitted to give away any of your property, or if any of your other gifts should fail for any reason.

Depending on your particular circumstances, you may want to

include additional provisions in your will, such as a guardianship clause, trust clause for your minor children, a simultaneous death clause, or predeceased clause in case a beneficiary should predecease you.

The guardianship clause nominates someone whom you would like to act as guardian of your minor children. The trust clause provides the terms and conditions as to how a gift to your minor children will be held and distributed. In the trust clause, you should appoint a trustee and give instructions as to how the trustee should distribute the gifts. The simultaneous death clause provides that, if you and a beneficiary should die together, the gift to that beneficiary will pass through your estate rather than the estate of the beneficiary. The predeceased clause provides that, if beneficiaries should die before you, their gifts will pass to their lawful descendants who survive you. Otherwise the gifts become part of your residuary estate. You may also want to include a pledge of your body or organs in your will.

You can revoke your will at any time before your death. You can revoke your will by tearing, canceling, burning, or otherwise destroying it with the intent of revoking it. Your will can also be revoked by making a new will. Your new will can revoke the old one by explicit language of revocation or by conflicting provisions. The best ways of revoking a will are to execute a new will that expressly revokes the old one, or to cancel or otherwise revoke the will in the presence of witnesses.

PLANNING FOR PROBATE

Many people think of probate as a complex, costly, and time-consuming process. Anxiety about the probate process has caused a lot of people to look at alternatives to probate, such as setting up a living trust or holding joint property or other nonprobate assets. However, in some cases probate can be simple and relatively inexpensive, particularly with small estates of about $50,000 or less. It may be important to review your particular situation, and your estate-planning options, with a qualified attorney or estate planner to make sure that you make the best choices.

"Probate" is the legal process by which your estate is settled and the property of your estate distributed. In general, this process involves settling all of your accounts and debts, paying any applicable estate and inheritance taxes, and distributing your property to your beneficiaries or heirs.

Probate proceedings are generally held in the probate court in the county and state where you resided on the date of your death. If you do not leave a will, your estate will be administered and distributed according to the law of inheritance of your state. If you have prepared a will, it will be offered for probate and your estate will be administered according to your will.

Your will has no real effect until it has been probated. The procedures for probate of a will vary for each state, but they generally require the filing of a petition or application for probate with the probate court. Your will can be offered for probate by anyone who has an interest in your estate. If no will is involved, a petition for the appointment of an administrator and administration of your estate would have to be filed.

Obviously, you will not be handling the probate of your own estate after your death. Unless you make other very specific arrangements, someone will have to go through some form of probate of your estate. As you grow older, it is also likely that you will have to probate the estate of a deceased family member or friend.

The procedures for probating an estate are governed by the law of the state where the decedent was domiciled. If real estate is located in other states, supplementary probate proceedings may also be required in those states to settle title to any real estate.

Generally a sworn petition or application for probate is filed in the probate court of the country where the decedent had his or her last domicile. The petition or application may be filed by the executor or executrix, a beneficiary, an heir, a creditor, or anyone with a claim against or interest in the estate. The petition or application should include a copy of any will, the decedent's death certificate, and a list of decedent's surviving spouse, next of kin, and heirs at law known to the petitioner or applicant. Hearings are scheduled by the court to settle claims and approve the disposition of the estate assets. The petitioner/applicant is usually required to publish notice of the probate hearing in the newspaper and send notice to any person known to have an interest in the decedent's estate.

There are usually several types of probate proceedings, such as court-supervised, informal, and small estate administration. In supervised probate the court oversees nearly all of the probate proceedings, imposes significant reporting requirements, and requires court approval for selling or disposing of estate property. Supervised probate can be time-consuming and expensive, and is typically required for large estates or where there is conflict between the heirs or beneficiaries.

Informal or unsupervised probate requires little court involvement and must be specified in the decedent's will or agreed to by the heirs and beneficiaries. It is less costly and less time-consuming than the supervised probate, and can usually be handled without the necessity of hiring a lawyer. In many cases the probate clerk's office or registrar of wills may be willing to provide guidance in handling these probate matters.

Small estate administration is probably the best probate process in terms of costs, time, and simplicity. It is available when the value of the estate is comparatively small. Be sure to check the law in your state for the estate value limits for small estate administration. Small estate probate can usually be accomplished in one to three months, compared to a year or longer for supervised probate.

Although the procedures vary from state to state, other steps in the probate process involve the following:

- Having the court officially confirm the executor or executrix named in the will, or appointing an administrator if there is no will
- Notifying heirs, beneficiaries, creditors, and other affected parties about the probate proceeding

- Preparing an inventory and appraisal of the estate property and debts, and filing this with the probate court
- Paying the creditors, taxes, and other expenses associated with probating or administering the estate
- Preparing a final accounting of the value of the estate, which shows all assets, debts, taxes, and other expenses, and filing this with the probate court
- Distributing the remainder of the estate property to beneficiaries according to the will, or to the heirs according to state law if there is no will
- Closing the estate by filing an affidavit that the estate business is finished or obtaining a court order that the estate is closed

Although a vast majority of probate cases are routine and uncomplicated, the services of an experienced attorney may be needed in a complex probate. Typical attorneys' fees in probate cases range from about 3 percent to about 5 percent of the value of the estate. These legal and administrative fees are usually paid out of the proceeds of the decedent's estate.

Probate is not required if you pass away leaving only property which is classified as "nonprobate property." Nonprobate property includes property that you own in trust, property owned jointly with a right of survivorship, and life insurance and pension benefits which are paid to someone else as beneficiary.

Using a Living Trust as an Alternative to Probate

A living or "inter vivos" trust can be used to avoid a lot of the expenses, time, and procedures of probating your estate. Basically, a living trust is the establishment of a separate legal entity during your lifetime to hold, manage, and distribute property according to the terms of a trust agreement.

A living trust can serve important functions in planning your estate for both probate and tax purposes. If you retain the right to revoke the trust, your estate must pay federal estate taxes on the trust assets. Also, income that the revocable trust earns will be taxable to you even if this income is paid to someone else. Federal estate taxes can be avoided by making the trust irrevocable or revocable only upon the occurrence of an event outside of your control.

A trust is established when you transfer real estate or personal property to someone to act as trustee pursuant to a trust agreement. A valid trust requires that title to the trust property actually be transferred to the trust. This is generally done by transferring the property to the trustee with a designation such as "to Carl Battle, trustee." The requirements as to who can serve as a trustee are governed by the laws of your specific state. Generally, any person or entity that is capable of contracting can serve as trustee. The trustee usually is a bank, an insurance company, a certified public accountant, an attorney, or any other person competent in business affairs. In many states, you can be the maker (or "settlor") of the trust and also serve as trustee, provided that you are not the only beneficiary.

Assets that you transfer to a living trust are generally not included in your estate for probate purposes. Instead, the assets of your living trust are distributed by your trustee according to the terms of your trust agreement. Therefore, it is important that your trust provide for the disposition of trust property and income after your death, particularly if you are the trustee or the initial life beneficiary. If you are the trustee, it is also important that you have appointed an alternate trustee in case of your death so that the trust provisions can be carried out.

Any property can be transferred to your living trust, whether it is real or personal property. The trust agreement can also provide for additional property to be added to the trust in the future. Your living trust can also be coordinated with your will to avoid probate by providing that any property that would be probated shall be transferred to your living trust upon your death. The trust property should be handled separately from and not commingled with your individual property or the trust may be invalidated as a sham.

There are many tax and estate issues that may arise in setting up a trust. Complicated and difficult trust arrangement may require the assistance of an attorney or tax specialist.

CHAPTER 9

Understanding Your Social Security Benefits

ALMOST EVERY PERSON IN THE UNITED STATES IS EITHER PAYING Social Security taxes or getting Social Security benefits—or is related to someone who is. While many of us associate Social Security primarily with retirement, it also provides, among other things, vital income to families of workers who are disabled or who die before retirement age. More than 40 million Americans receive some form of a Social Security benefit. That figure equals about one out of every six Americans.

The Social Security system, created under the Social Security Act of 1935, was designed to "provide for the general welfare." It covers a broad range of programs, including retirement insurance, disability insurance, survivor's insurance, hospital and medical insurance for the aged and disabled, black lung benefits, Supplemental Security Income (SSI), unemployment insurance, and varied public assistance and "welfare" services. This chapter will focus mostly on the "typical" Social Security benefits, i.e., retirement, disability, survivor's, Medicare, and SSI benefits.

WHO PAYS SOCIAL SECURITY TAXES?

Employers, employees, and the self-employed pay Social Security and Medicare taxes commonly referred to as FICA. These taxes are used to pay for all Social Security benefits. Additionally, a portion of these taxes are used to pay for Medicare coverage. SSI is financed through general tax revenues, not Social Security taxes. Here's how it works.

If you work for someone else, you and your employer pay taxes for both Social Security and Medicare. In 1996, you and your employer each paid 7.65 percent of your gross salary, up to a limit established by an act of Congress or by a formula tied to cost-of-living increases in Social Security benefits. In 1996, the limit was $62,700 for the payment of Social Security taxes. For planning purposes, keep in mind that the tax and earnings bases are generally announced in October or November of the year prior to the year in which the increase is to take effect.

The 7.65 percent represents a combination of two rates: the Social Security rate (6.20 percent) and the Medicare (hospital insurance) rate (1.45 percent). Unlike the Social Security part of the tax, you will continue to pay the Medicare portion of the FICA tax on earnings above the Social Security tax limit.

If you work for yourself, you pay 15.3 percent of your taxable income in FICA taxes, up to the prescribed limit. As a general rule, self-employment income would be your net earnings from a trade or business carried on as a sole proprietor or as a member of a partnership. Usually, the same limits on taxable income that apply to wage earners also apply to the self-employed, with some exceptions. If you are self-employed, there are special deductions intended to offset your tax rate that you can take when filing your tax return. You should consult a competent tax advisor on this subject, if you have questions after reading IRS Form 1040 instructions or reviewing Social Security's fact sheet, *If You're Self-Employed* (Publication No. 05-10022).

WHAT DOES SOCIAL SECURITY COVER?

The major programs covered by the U.S. Social Security system are retirement, disability, survivors, Medicare, and SSI. Let's take a look at the specific benefits offered under Social Security.

Retirement Benefits

Full Retirement You will be eligible for your full Social Security benefit at the age of sixty-five, if you were born before 1938. However, if you were born in 1938 or later, you will be subject to the 1983 amendments to the Social Security Act. As a result of these amendments, beginning in the year 2000, the age at which full benefits are payable will increase in gradual steps from age sixty-five to age sixty-seven.

The following table from the Social Security Administration shows how the full retirement age will increase:

Age to Receive Full Social Security Benefits

YEAR OF BIRTH	FULL RETIREMENT AGE
1937 or earlier	65
1938	65 + 2 months
1939	65 + 4 months
1940	65 + 6 months
1941	65 + 8 months
1942	65 + 10 months
1943–54	66
1955	66 + 2 months
1956	66 + 4 months
1957	66 + 6 months
1958	66 + 8 months
1959	66 + 10 months
1960 or later	67

Reduced Benefit for Early Retirement Regardless of what your "full" retirement age is, you may start receiving benefits as early as age sixty-two. But, if you start your benefits early, they will be reduced a small percentage based on the number of months you will receive checks before you reach full retirement age. For example, if your full retirement age is sixty-five, the reduction for starting your Social Security benefit at age sixty-two is 20 percent; at age sixty-three, it is 13⅓ percent; and at age sixty-four, it is 6⅔ percent.

If you were born after 1937, thereby making your full retirement age older than sixty-five, you still will be able to take your retirement benefits at age sixty-two, but the reduction in your benefit amount will be greater than it is for people retiring now. For example, someone retiring at age sixty-two now will receive thirty-six months' benefits before reaching the full retirement age of sixty-five, resulting in a 20 percent reduction. An individual whose full retirement age is sixty-seven will receive benefits for sixty months between age sixty-two and full retirement age. This result is a 30 percent reduction. The general rule is that early retirement will give you about the same total Social Security benefits over your lifetime, but in smaller amounts to account for the longer period you will receive them.

Poor health causes some people to retire early. If poor health keeps you from continuing your work, consider applying for Social Security disability. The disability benefit amount is the same as a full, unreduced retirement benefit. You should contact Social Security for more information on this subject.

Delayed or Late Retirement If you decide to continue working full-time beyond your full retirement age and, accordingly, do not sign up for Social Security until later, you can increase your Social Security benefit in two ways. First, your extra income will generally increase your "average" earnings, which is the basis for determining the amount of your retirement benefit. It follows that the higher your average earnings, the higher your Social Security benefit will be. Second, your Social Security benefit will be increased by a certain percentage if you delay retirement. This special credit varies depending on your date of birth. The increases will be added automatically from the time full retirement age is reached until you start taking your benefits, or you reach age seventy. The chart below shows the increase that applies to you:

Chart of Increases for Delayed or Late Retirement

YEAR OF BIRTH	YEARLY INCREASE
1916 or earlier	1.0%
1917–24	3.0%
1925–26	3.5%
1927–28	4.0%
1929–30	4.5%
1931–32	5.0%
1933–34	5.5%
1935–36	6.0%
1937–38	6.5%
1939–40	7.0%
1941–42	7.5%
1943 or later	8.0%

As an example, if you were born in 1943 or later, Social Security will add an extra 8 percent to your benefit for each year you delay signing up for Social Security beyond your full retirement age. The 8 percent per year impacts people turning age sixty-five in the year 2008 or later.

Disability Benefits under Social Security

Although the dictionary defines "disability" as "a physical or mental condition that prevents a person from leading a normal life," the Social Security definition of disability is more specific and is generally related to your ability to work. In order to qualify for a Social Security disability, you must have a physical or mental impairment that is expected to keep you from doing any "substantial" work for at least one year (as a general rule, monthly earnings of $500 or more are considered substantial). Alternatively, you must have a condition that is expected to result in death. Social

Security is not intended for temporary conditions or "partial" disabilities. In order to qualify for disability benefits, you must have earned a minimum number of quarters of Social Security coverage (as defined later in this chapter), subject to certain rules about earning some of these quarters in recent years.

Social Security benefits can be received at any age. If you are getting disability benefits at age sixty-five, they will become retirement benefits, although the amount remains the same. If you retire or become disabled certain members of your family may also qualify for benefits based on your Social Security record. These family members include:

- Your unmarried son or daughter, including a stepchild, adopted child, or, in some cases, a grandchild. The child must be under eighteen or under nineteen if in high school full time
- Your unmarried son or daughter, eighteen or older, if he or she has a disability that started before twenty-two (If a disabled child under eighteen is receiving benefits as a dependent of a retired, deceased, or disabled worker, Social Security should be contacted to have his or her checks continued at eighteen on the basis of disability)
- Your spouse who is sixty-two or older
- Your spouse at any age if he or she is caring for a child of yours who is under sixteen or disabled and also receiving checks

In the event of your death, certain family members may qualify for disability benefits, such as:

- Your disabled widow or widower fifty or older (The disability must have started before your death or within seven years after your death)
- If your widow or widower caring for your children receives Social Security benefits, she or he is eligible if she or he becomes disabled before those payments end or within seven years after they end
- Your disabled ex-wife or husband who is fifty or older, if the marriage lasted ten years or longer

Since disability is one of the most complicated of all Social Security programs, you should call or visit your Social Security office to get more information.

Individuals with HIV infection or AIDS may also qualify for disability benefits under two sets of circumstances: (1) when, because of the disease, they must severely limit the amount of work they do and (2) when they are no longer able to work. For more information on this subject, you should request the booklet, *A Guide to Social Security and SSI Disability Benefits For People With HIV Infection* (Publication No. 05-10020) or contact your Social Security office.

Supplemental Security Income Benefits

Supplemental Security Income, generally called "SSI," is a program administered by Social Security, but for which benefits are financed by the general revenue funds of the U.S. Treasury. Benefits do not come from Social Security taxes or Social Security trust funds.

SSI makes monthly payments to people who are sixty-five or older, blind, or have a disability, and who have low incomes and few assets. Children and adults are eligible for SSI benefits because of blindness or disability. On occasion, a person whose sight is not poor enough to be considered blind may be able to get benefits as a disabled person. Additionally, to get SSI you generally must reside in the United States and be a U.S. citizen or be an alien living in the U.S. legally.

Eligibility for SSI also depends on what you own and how much income you have. The word "income" in this context means money you have coming in as wages, Social Security checks, and pensions. Further, it means "noncash" items you receive such as the value of food, clothing, and shelter.

If you are married, Social Security will also look at the income of your spouse and the things he or she owns. If you are under eighteen, it may look at the income of your parents and the things they own. Similarly, if you are a sponsored alien, Social Security may look at the income of your sponsor and what he or she owns.

The amount of income you can have and still receive SSI benefits depends on whether you work and the state in which you live. While there is a basic national payment, some states add money to the national payment, resulting in higher SSI rates and higher income limits than others. You can contact Social Security to find out the income limits in your state.

An individual may be able to get SSI if the assets counted by Social Security are no more than $2,000 for one person, or $3,000 for a couple. These limits do not change from state to state as they do in the income category.

Assets (the things you own) that are considered by Social Security in determining your eligibility for SSI include items such as real estate, personal belongings, bank accounts, cash, and stocks and bonds. However, Social Security does not count everything you own. For example, Social Security does not include the following:

- The home you live in and the land it is on
- Your personal and household goods up to a limit of $2,000 in total value
- Your car (generally)
- Burial plots for you and immediate family members
- Up to $1,500 in burial funds for you and your spouse
- The cash value of life insurance policies with face values of $1,500 or less
- If you are blind or have a disability, some items may not count if you plan to use them to work or earn extra income

The majority of individuals who receive SSI can also get food stamps and Medicaid assistance. Remember that Medicaid helps pay doctor and hospital bills. You should contact Social Security for information on nutrition programs and a local social services office for more information about Medicaid. Also, see chapter 5 for a discussion on the Medicaid program and chapter 7 for advice on how to manage your assets to maximize benefit under Social Security and Medicaid.

Medicare Benefits

As described earlier, Medicare is the U.S.'s health insurance program for people sixty-five or older, certain disabled individuals under sixty-five, and people of any age who have permanent kidney failure, and it provides basic protection against the cost of health care. Since the subject of Medicare is covered in chapter 5, only a brief overview will be provided here.

There are two parts to Medicare:

- *Hospital Insurance* (also called "Part A") helps pay for inpatient hospital care, and certain followup services
- *Medical Insurance* (also called "Part B") helps pay for doctor's service, outpatient hospital care, and certain related medical services

As a general rule, Part A of Medicare is financed by payroll and self-employment taxes. Part B is financed by monthly premiums from those who enroll and partially by the general revenues of the federal government. Part A benefits are provided on the basis of past work, while Part B benefits are provided only if you pay the monthly premiums.

Virtually everyone who is eligible for Part A through a work record, a spouse's record, or payment of the Medicare tax as a government employee, can sign up for Part B. Part B is an optional program which requires the payment of monthly premiums. Part A is free when you are eligible for it, since it was paid for by your taxes while you worked.

Survivors' Benefits under Social Security

Survivors' benefits are those benefits that certain members of your family may be eligible for upon your death based on your Social Security record. Family members who can receive Social Security benefits include the surviving spouse and ex-spouse, children, and dependent parents, all of whom must meet certain requirements.

A special one-time lump sum death benefit of $255 is payable to your surviving spouse who was living with you at the time of your death. If there is no spouse living with you, the lump sum payment can be made only to certain members of your family.

The lump sum benefit is made in addition to, and does not affect, monthly benefits to which the widow or widower may be entitled. If there are no eligible survivors, the benefit is not paid.

Benefits for Your Family

Once you start collecting Social Security retirement or disability benefits, other members of your family may also be eligible for payments, including your spouse, children, grandchildren, and divorced spouse. As a general rule, a spouse and other dependents will be eligible for a monthly benefit that is up to 50 percent of your retirement or disability benefit, subject to a maximum family benefit.

The Social Security law places a limit on the amount of money that can be paid to your family based on your Social Security record. The limit is generally equal to about 150 to 180 percent of your retirement benefit. The range may be lower for disability benefits. Where the sum of the benefits payable on your account is greater than the maximum family benefit, the benefits to your family will be reduced proportionately to bring the total within the limit. However, other benefits will not be affected. The benefit payable to a divorced spouse is not included in your maximum family benefit calculation, except for a surviving divorced spouse who qualifies only on the basis of caring for your child.

WHEN WILL YOU QUALIFY FOR SOCIAL SECURITY BENEFITS?

Social Security work credits are earned as you work and pay taxes. They are generally the prerequisites to getting benefits out of the system. An exception to this general rule is that some people can get benefits as a dependent or survivor on another person's Social Security record.

Most people earn four credits per year, which is the maximum that can be earned in one year. In 1996, workers earned one credit for each $640 in earnings. Every year, the amount of money needed to earn one credit is adjusted. The number of credits needed to qualify for Social Security depends on your age and the type of benefit for which you might be eligible. The majority of people need forty credits (ten years of work) to qualify for benefits. Fewer credits are needed by young people to be eligible for disability benefits or for their dependents to be eligible for survivors' benefits if they should die.

It is likely that you will earn more credits than you need during your working lifetime to be eligible for Social Security. While the extra credits themselves will not increase your Social Security benefit, the income you earn while working will increase your benefit. Generally, citizens and those with lawful alien status will earn credits toward qualification for benefits for all services performed in the United States, regardless of the citizenship or residence of either the employee or employer. Qualification will be based on work credits as discussed earlier in this chapter.

If you work outside the United States, special rules apply. For more information, contact your Social Security office regarding any totalization agreement, which is a bilateral arrangement between the United States and a foreign country that prevents double Social Security taxation of U.S. citizens employed abroad and that assures continuity of coverage for U.S. citizens who divide their working careers between work covered by the U.S. Social Security system and by a foreign Social Security or pension system. U.S. citizens can travel or live in most foreign countries without affecting their eligibility for Social Security benefits. You should note that there are a few countries, such as Albania and Cuba, where Social Security checks cannot be sent.

Note that if you did not work long enough to qualify for Social Security, or if you receive only a minimal benefit, you may be eligible for SSI discussed earlier in this chapter.

HOW AND WHEN DO YOU APPLY FOR SOCIAL SECURITY?

You must apply to receive Social Security benefits because the government will not automatically do it for you. An application for benefits can be made at any Social Security office. Social Security has about 1,300 offices in cities and towns across the United States. You can visit the office nearest you or you can call 1-800-772-1213 from 7:00 A.M. to 7:00 P.M. every business day. Check telephone listings under "U.S. Government" for your local Social Security office. The easiest way to file a claim is to call the toll-free number ahead of time for an appointment.

You should apply for disability, survivor's, and SSI benefits as soon as you are eligible. The Social Security Administration suggests that you sign up for retirement benefits three months before you want your benefits to start.

Some of the records you may be asked to provide, depending on your claim, include:

- Your Social Security card or a record of your number
- Your birth certificate
- Children's birth certificates or adoption papers and Social Security numbers if they are applying
- Your most recent W-2 form, or your tax return if you are self-employed
- Worker's death certificate
- Proof that the deceased supported you, if you are a dependent

Even if you do not have all the documents you need, do not delay signing up for Social Security benefits. The Social Security Administration will help you get the needed information or advise you of other acceptable proof.

Your Social Security or SSI payments can either be deposited directly into your bank account or sent to you in the mail. In addition to being safer and more convenient than checks, direct deposit is more efficient and saves money for the federal government. In order to choose direct deposit, have your checkbook or any papers that show your bank account number with you when you sign up for Social Security.

How Much Will Your Benefit Be?

Your Social Security benefit is based on factors such as your date of birth, the type of benefit for which you are applying, and your earnings averaged over most of your working life. The easiest way to find out the benefits you will receive is by contacting the Social Security Administration. The Social Security Administration will provide you with a detailed, written personal estimate of your retirement, disability, and survivors benefits upon your request. Ask for Form SSA-7004 (Request for Earnings and Benefit Estimate Statement).

In about six weeks or less, you will receive a statement that will indicate the following:

- The number of credits that you have earned
- The number of credits that you still need to earn to receive retirement, disability, and survivor's benefits
- A list of your earnings subject to Social Security tax, as well as your Social Security tax payments by year
- Estimates of your monthly retirement benefits at ages sixty-two, sixty-five, and seventy
- Estimates of disability and survivor's benefits for you and your dependents

Although it is your employer's responsibility to submit Social Security taxes on your behalf, you should periodically check your earnings record to make sure there are no mistakes. Sometimes, an employer may forget to submit the payroll taxes. Or, if you have changed your name, your earnings may be mistakenly posted to someone else's record. In any case, it is a good habit to check your record every two or three years. It is a simple and painless procedure that could prevent you from losing many thousands of dollars in benefits.

DEFENDING YOUR RIGHTS TO SOCIAL SECURITY BENEFITS

When the Social Security Administration makes a decision that affects your eligibility for Social Security or SSI benefits, it will send you a letter that explains the decision. If you disagree with the decision, you have the right to appeal it and ask the Social Security Administration to reconsider your case. This request must be submitted within sixty days after the date of the initial determination by either completing a "Request for Reconsideration Form" or by writing a letter to any Social Security Office.

The appeals process within the Social Security system involves three steps. If you are unsuccessful after these steps, your fourth step would be to bring a civil case in the federal courts. The complete appeal process is given below:

1. Reconsideration by the Social Security Administration
2. Hearing before an administrative law judge or hearing examiner
3. Review by an appeals council established within the Social Security Administration
4. Requesting a federal court hearing

You have sixty days from the time you receive the decision to file an appeal to the next level. Social Security assumes that you received the decision five days after the date on it, unless you can show that you received it later. You have the right to be represented by a qualified person (including an attorney) of your choice when dealing with the Social Security Administration.

For additional information, call or visit any Social Security Office to ask for a copy of the following fact sheets: *The Appeals Process* (Publication No. 05-10041) and *Social Security and Your Right to Representation* (Publication No. 05-10075).

WILL YOUR SOCIAL SECURITY BENEFIT BE TAXED?

Some people who get Social Security will have to pay taxes on their benefits. Those impacted are people in higher income tax brackets. However, no more than one-half of the Social Security benefit will be taxed. For a federal tax return filed as an "individual," you may have to pay taxes on 50 percent of your Social Security benefits if your combined income is between $25,000 to $34,000. For a federal tax return filed jointly, you may have to pay taxes on your Social Security benefits if your combined income is between $32,000 to $44,000. The term "combined income" is defined as your and your spouse's adjusted gross income (from your Form 1040) plus nontaxable interest and one-half of your Social Security benefits.

The tax is on 85 percent of your Social Security benefit if your combined income is above $34,000 and $44,000 for individual and joint filings, respectively.

WORKING WHILE RECEIVING SOCIAL SECURITY

The Social Security Act limits the amount of money you can earn and continue to receive all of your Social Security retirement benefits. This restriction, often referred to as a retirement earnings test or earnings limit, impacts people under the age of seventy who collect Social Security retirement, as well as the benefits of dependents and survivors. After 1982, persons age seventy and older are allowed unlimited earnings without any loss of benefits under the annual earnings test. Individuals who work and collect disability or SSI benefits have different earnings requirements.

For example, in 1996, you could earn up to $8,280 and still collect all of your Social Security retirement benefits, if you are under age sixty-five. For every $2 earned over the limit, $1 would be withheld from your benefit. For those ages sixty-five through sixty-nine, you could earn up to $12,500 and still collect all of your Social Security retirement benefits. For every $3 earned over the limit, $1 would be withheld from your Social Security benefit.

Earnings included for this purpose are income from a job or the net profit from self-employment. Bonuses, commissions, and vacation pay are counted. However, the following items are not counted as earned income: pensions, annuities, investment income, interest, and Social Security, veteran's, and other government benefits.

Other Information Concerning Social Security

Once you start collecting benefits, you should let Social Security know when events occur that could affect your benefits. Examples include:

- Moving
- Getting married or divorced
- Changing your name
- An income or earnings change
- Birth or adoption of a child
- Imprisonment of a beneficiary
- Leaving the United States
- Death of a beneficiary

If you are unable to manage your financial affairs, Social Security, following a careful investigation, will appoint a relative, friend, or another interested party to handle your Social Security matters. This individual is referred to as your "representative payee." Your Social Security benefits will be made payable in the representative payee's name on your behalf.

CHAPTER 10

Reviewing Your Pension Benefits

WITH ALMOST 60 PERCENT OF THE WORKERS IN THE UNITED STATES covered by private pensions, you can easily see that your pension is an important financial resource for your retirement years. In fact, your pension, personal annuities and savings, and Social Security benefits are likely to be the only sources of income after you retire. Therefore, it is important that you understand if and when you are covered by a pension plan and to what benefits you may be entitled.

You need to know whether your employer has a pension plan. Employers are not required to have pension plans for their employees, although most large and medium-sized companies do. You also need to know if you are specifically covered by your employer's pension plan, because it is not required that all employees be included.

A pension is basically a program under which your employer or union contributes money to a fund during your years of work to provide income to you after you retire. Your pension differs from an Individual Retirement Arrangement (IRA) or private annuity in that a pension is generally employer financed, while you typically fund and maintain your IRA and other private annuities.

Your Pension Rights under Federal Laws

Although your employer does not have to set up a pension plan, if one is set up, it must meet certain federal requirements. Most of the required standards for pension plans are provided by the federal Employee Retirement Income Security Act (ERISA). Exempt from ERISA are certain governmental plans, church plans, and other special plans for workers' compensation, unemployment compensation, or disability. Additional rules apply to pension plans under the Labor Management Relations Act (covering union members), the Age Discrimination in Employment Act of 1967 (prohibiting age discrimination), the Civil Rights Act of 1964, and the federal tax laws. Your rights as a pension plan participant are generally defined in Title I of ERISA.

Your employer's pension plan may not cover all employees. The pension laws and regulations allow employers to include or exclude certain categories of employees from a pension plan, provided that the plan does not discriminate in favor of shareholders, officers, and other highly-paid employees.

ERISA does not apply to small employers having less than twenty-five employees. If you are covered by a pension plan which is not regulated by ERISA, you must rely on your plan documents for your rights to pension benefits.

Requirements for Participating in a Pension Plan

Under the ERISA laws, employees who are at least twenty-one years old and have worked for their employer for at least one year typically must be allowed to participate in the employer's pension plan. There are several exceptions for schools, plans providing full vesting after three years, and other special situations. The one-year requirement for participation in a pension plan can generally be met by twelve months of continuous full- or part-time employment or employment for one thousand hours in a twelve-month period.

Certain pension plans which provide for a fixed amount to be paid to employees (for example, $1,000 per month for each year of service) may require five years of service prior to retirement before you can collect a pension. These are called "defined benefits" plans and are the most common pension plans.

Another type of pension plan is the "defined contribution" plan wherein your employer contributes a fixed amount into the pension plan for each year of your service. Your retirement benefits under a defined contribution will depend on the amount of your employer's contributions and how well the plan performs over your work life.

Pension plans may not exclude an employee solely on the basis of part-time or seasonal employment if the employee has a "year of service" as defined by ERISA. Generally, a year of service is one thousand hours of service during a twelve-month period. Plans of the maritime industry may designate 125 days as constituting a year of service. In the case of a seasonal industry where the customary period of employment is less than one thousand hours during the year, a year of service is to be defined by regulation.

There are other circumstances where an employee who may have less than one thousand hours of service must be deemed to have completed a "year of service." Some plans, instead of counting all hours of service from records, use an equivalency permitted by regulations to determine hours of service. In such cases, employees who meet specified requirements must be treated as having the equivalent to 1,000 hours of service even though they may not actually have 1,000 hours of service. Plans which use another alternative method of crediting service (called "elapsed time") base eligibility to participate on whether one year has elapsed while the employee is employed with the employer, irrespective of the number of hours of service completed.

Participation cannot be denied an employee because he or she begins employment late in life if the plan provides defined contributions such as profit sharing, stock bonus, or money purchase plans. Plans providing defined benefits (not contributions) are permitted to exclude from pension plan participation an employee who begins employment within five years of the plan's normal retirement age. However, for plan years starting on or after January 1, 1988, employers no longer will be able to exclude from plan participation employees who start work within five years of a plan's normal retirement age. For collectively bargained plans, this rule is effective on the earlier of (1) the later of January 1, 1988, or the date on which the last of the contracts expires, or (2) January 1, 1990. A "floating" normal retirement age, which could be no later than the fifth anniversary of the employee's participation in the plan, could be established.

After you have met the requirements for participation in a pension plan you begin to accumulate benefits toward retirement. The amount of your retirement benefits are normally determined by the number of years you have worked with your employer.

Becoming Vested Under a Pension Plan

Although you accrue retirement benefits while participating in a pension plan, you do not have a right to these benefits unless they are vested. Accruing benefits over long periods means little if you can lose these benefits. Accordingly, through its vesting provisions, ERISA assures employees who work for a specified minimum period under a pension plan of at least some pension at retirement. ERISA's vesting provisions generally did not become effective until the first day of 1976. If your service ended before that date, your rights would be governed by the rules of your plan.

When you become vested in your pension plan, you have a legal right to receive a pension at retirement age under your plan. Vesting is different from participating because vesting guarantees your right to a pension. Participating means only that you have qualified to be a part of the plan. For example, you might begin participating in a pension plan after one year of service, but the plan might provide that you work for five years before you become vested. This would mean that if you left the employer at any time before five years of service, you would not be vested and therefore would receive no pension benefits.

The ERISA laws establish minimum vesting requirements for pension plans. Before 1976 pension plans could require you to work your whole life for one employer before any pension benefits were vested. From 1976 to 1989 the typical vesting requirement was ten years of service. Since 1989 pension plans are required to provide minimum vesting under either a five-year, 100 percent vesting rule, or a seven-year, graded vesting rule. Remember different vesting rules apply to people who stopped working under a pension plan before 1989. The five-year, 100 percent rule requires that employees be fully vested after five years of service. The seven-year rule requires that employees be vested according to the following schedule: 20 percent after three years, 40 percent after four years, 60 percent after five years, 80 percent after six years, and 100 percent after seven years. Some union-negotiated pension plans paid for by more than one company can follow a ten-year, 100 percent vesting rule where employees are fully vested after ten years of service. Pension plans can provide for more rapid vesting schedules than those required by ERISA.

COUNTING YOUR YEARS OF SERVICE

Your rights with respect to participation, vesting, and benefit accrual are generally determined by reference to years of service and years of participation completed by you and any breaks in service incurred. Whether an employee has completed a year of service is generally measured in terms of the number of hours of service credited to the employee during a twelve-consecutive-month period designated by the plan.

It is important to examine your plan documents carefully so you will know exactly what "service" is counted in determining a "year of service" and "years of participation" under your plan and what periods are not counted for participation, vesting, and benefit accrual. You need to know this so you will not inadvertently incur a break in service or fail to participate, accrue benefits, or have periods counted for vesting.

ERISA and its regulations set minimum standards for defining "years of service" and "hour of service" under pension plans. These are minimum standards only, so plans may define these terms more liberally to benefit you. ERISA defines "year of service" for purposes of participation and vesting as a twelve-month period during which an employee has one thousand hours of service. An employee who works an average of twenty hours a week will have over one thousand hours of service in a year. Remember, in the maritime industry 125 days may be designated as constituting a year of service and, in the case of seasonal industries, ERISA specifies that "year of service" be defined by regulation.

ERISA also protects you from loss of pension benefits because of short breaks in service. As a general rule for vesting purposes you must be credited with a year of service for each year that you work one thousand hours or more. Every hour for which you are paid counts toward the one thousand–hour requirement, including vacation days, sick days, personal days, and holidays.

Pension plans are also allowed to calculate years of service by counting your continuous years of employment from your date of hire. If you are laid off or disabled under this plan, you must be given vesting credit for one year after your date of layoff or disability.

In determining your rights to pension benefits, your employer usually must give you credit for all the years you worked for your employer after age eighteen. You must also be given credit for the time you were in the military service if you returned to the same job after leaving the military.

ERISA also provides that the employer credit you for years worked before a break in service if you were away from that employer for less than five consecutive years. This five-year break in service rule does not cause you to lose credit for the years you left because of pregnancy or to take care of a newborn child, or for years in which you worked more than five hundred hours for the employer.

If your pension plan requires ten years for vesting, you generally must be credited with prior years worked if your break in service was less than the time you worked for the employer before the break.

Even with the break-in-service rules discussed earlier, your employer may require that you work at least one year after the break to receive credit for previous years.

Protection from Pension Plan Amendments, Terminations, and Mergers

If you have vested rights under a pension plan, you will not lose these rights if you leave your employer for any reason. You keep your vested benefits even if you leave to work for a competitor or other employer. Your employer is also prohibited from amending its pension plan to take away your accrued or vested benefit.

Your employer can make changes to its pension plan if the changes do not affect your accrued or vested benefits. Also any changes to the plan would generally only apply to the years after the change and not to the years you have already worked.

Some of your pension benefits are protected even if your employer terminated the pension plan, or goes out of business because of financial problems. Nearly all employees covered by defined benefits plans are protected by insurance under the Pension Benefit Guaranty Corporation (PBGC). The PBGC insurance only protects vested benefits, so you are not protected if you have not vested under your pension plan. Additionally, PBGC insurance protects only your basic retirement benefits up to a maximum amount, but not many of the special benefits you may have under your pension plan.

For further information on plan termination insurance, you should write to the PBGC. The address is 2020 K Street, N.W., Washington, DC 20006, Attention: Coverage and Inquiries Branch.

The Internal Revenue Code also provides some protection in the event of a termination or partial termination of a tax-qualified retirement plan. The Internal Revenue Code provides for full and immediate vesting of all accrued benefits, to the extent then funded, upon the complete or partial termination of a tax-qualified plan. However, benefits vested solely because of the termination or partial termination of a plan, rather than because of completion of the required number of years of service, are not guaranteed by the PBGC. Therefore, whether benefits vested in the event of a termination or partial termination will actually be paid depends on whether the plan is sufficiently funded to pay those benefits.

If you are covered by a "defined contribution" pension plan, it is not insured by PBGC. If your plan terminates, you will be paid whatever funds are in your account. If your pension plan was started within the five years before the plan was terminated, then your benefits may not be insured. Also, if your pension plan was improved within five years before it was terminated, these improvements might not be insured. Lump sum death benefits and disability benefits are usually not insured. Additionally, the PBGC insurance generally provides maximum age sixty-five benefits of only about $2,000 per month.

If your pension plan is terminated for any reason other than financial problems, you will get all of the benefits you have earned under the plan. If your total benefits are $3,500 or less, you are likely to be paid in a lump sum after the plan is terminated. Otherwise the pension plan funds are generally used to purchase insurance annuities that will pay your pension benefits when you retire.

In the case of a merger or consolidation of plans or a transfer of assets or liabilities from one plan to any other plan, each participant must be entitled to receive a benefit after the merger which is at least equal to the value of the benefit he or she would have been entitled to receive before the merger. The before-and-after merger benefits are determined as if the plan had been terminated.

ERISA also protects participants of certain pension plans from financing which is inadequate to pay the promised benefits. In order to make sure that sufficient money is available to pay promised pension benefits to employees when they retire, ERISA sets down rules for funding pension plans. Funding is monitored by actuaries and adjusted every three years to assure the soundness of plans.

ERISA protects employee pension plans from financial losses caused by mismanagement and misuse of assets through its fiduciary provisions. A fiduciary who breaches any responsibility or duty under ERISA may be personally liable to make good any losses to the plan resulting from such a breach and to restore to the plan any profits made through improper use of plan assets. A fiduciary is also subject to such other equitable or remedial relief as a court may deem appropriate, including removal.

PAYMENT OF YOUR PENSION

The normal retirement age under most pension plans is age sixty-five, and you are likely to receive maximum benefits when you retire at that age. If you retire before age sixty-five, your pension benefits will probably be reduced under most plans. If you continue to work under your pension plan after age sixty-five, federal law requires that you be paid a pension by April 1 of the year after you turn seventy-and-one-half.

Your pension benefits are normally paid to you after your retirement as a monthly amount for the rest of your life. Some pension plans may allow you to elect other payment methods, such as a lump sum or payment over a certain period of time.

Your pension benefits normally stop upon your death, except that your spouse is entitled to receive a part of your benefits. Your spouse will typically receive for life one-half of your vested pension benefits, unless you and your spouse jointly have elected another alternative. A spouse is entitled to continue to receive benefits even after remarriage. You and your spouse can waive these surviving spouse benefits in writing. If you are unmarried at the time of your death, no pension benefits are required to be paid unless your pension plan specifically provides for such.

If you are divorced, your ex-spouse may still be entitled to a part of your pension benefits. Your pension benefits are considered as marital property in most states. They can be divided at divorce by court order and your pension plan can be required to pay a portion to your ex-spouse.

You retain your vested rights to a pension even if you are covered by another pension plan, profit-sharing plan, IRA, or Social Security. However, some pension plans reduce your pension benefits based on the amount you will receive as Social Security. For service after 1989, the reduction for Social Security can not exceed 50 percent of your pension benefits.

Your pension benefits are not reduced because of unemployment payments that you are receiving. However, if you are collecting workers' compensation, your pension payments can be reduced.

Obtaining Information on Your Pension Plan

ERISA requires plan administrators—the people who run pension plans—to give you in writing the most important facts you need to know about your plan. They must also provide you plan documents at reasonable cost if you make a written request.

ERISA requires that plan information be disclosed to participants and, in some cases, their beneficiaries, as well as to the government. Most plans are required to file financial reports with the IRS and summary plan descriptions with the U.S. Department of Labor.

The summary plan description must be furnished to participants and beneficiaries. It must give information on what the plan provides and how it operates. It also must be written in a manner to be understood by the average plan participant and, in an accurate and comprehensive manner, advise participants of their rights and entitlements.

The administrator must furnish automatically to participants and beneficiaries receiving benefits information such as the summary plan description, summaries of any changes, and a summary of the annual report. If requested in writing, the administrator must furnish to any pension plan participant or beneficiary a statement of total benefits accrued, accrued benefits which are vested, if any, or the earliest date on which the accrued benefits will become vested. This statement need not be furnished more than once in a twelve-month period.

Plans must also respond to written benefit claims. If a claim for benefits is denied in whole or in part, the administrator must write to the participant or beneficiary to explain why the benefits were denied and advise how the denial may be appealed.

Be sure to retain copies of your pension plan summary, benefit statements, detailed pension plan document, and any other agreements relating to your employment. Understand what benefits you have earned and can count on for your retirement years. See your plan administrator, personnel officer, or a pension benefits lawyer if you need assistance.

Filing a Claim for Your Pension

Employee benefit plans must have a reasonable and written procedure for processing written claims for benefits and for appeals if the original claim is denied. Therefore, if you believe you are entitled to a benefit from a pension or welfare benefit plan, you should write to the administrator of your plan to file a claim.

If a claim for benefits is denied, the participant must be notified in writing (generally within ninety days after the claim is filed) of the reason(s) for the denial and the specific plan provisions on which the denial is based. Any notice of denial must also tell you what additional information may be required in order to perfect your claim and find out how to appeal the denial.

You have at least ninety days in which to appeal a denial. A decision on your appeal generally must be made within sixty days, unless the plan provides for a special hearing or the decision must be made by a group which meets only on a periodic basis. The decision on review must be furnished to the claimant and include the reasons for the decision, together with references to plan documents.

If your claim is denied and you believe you are entitled to benefits, you may wish to write to the plan administrator to request a copy of the complete plan rules. A reasonable charge (up to twenty-five cents a page) may be made for copies of the plan rules. You could then compare the plan rules with the plan provisions cited by the plan in the denial to determine whether the rules have been properly applied.

You should consult your summary plan description if you have any questions about how your plan processes claims.

Other Retirement Plans

In addition to your regular employer-sponsored pension plan, there are a variety of other retirement arrangements you might want to consider. Arrangements such as an Individual Retirement Account (IRA) or 401(k) plan may be invaluable as an additional source of retirement income.

Under the tax laws beginning in 1987, certain people can open or continue to contribute to IRAs. The amount contributed may be claimed as a deduction on your federal income tax return. Earnings on your IRA contributions are not taxable until you begin withdrawing benefits at age fifty-nine-and-one-half or later. Therefore, you may contribute to your own retirement plan and have earnings on those contributions accumulate on a tax-free basis. When you begin to withdraw the accumulated funds, the benefits will be taxable but you may be in a lower tax bracket than when you were employed.

Deductible IRA contributions are permitted unless (1) an individual or married couple has an adjusted gross income (AGI) above a specified phase-out level, or (2) the individual (or, if married, either the individual or the spouse) is an active participant in an employer-maintained retirement plan for any part of the plan year ending with or within the individual's taxable year. Individuals may make nondeductible IRA contributions to the extent they are not eligible to make deductible contributions and earnings on such contributions are not subject to tax until they are withdrawn.

If you receive a lump sum payment from a tax-qualified pension plan due to retirement, disability, termination of your employment, or termination of your pension plan, you may be able to defer taxes by depositing the funds in an IRA. This is called tax-free rollover. Later, you could transfer this sum tax-free to a new employer's pension plan if the plan permits it.

The rules governing IRAs are administered by the IRS. For further information, contact the nearest IRS office listed in your local telephone directory. PBGC also gives advice and assistance on evaluating the economic desirability of establishing IRAs and rollovers. For a copy of their booklet on IRAs, write to PBGC, Coverage and Inquiries Branch, 2020 K Street, N.W., Washington, DC 20006.

The tax laws also allow employers to establish a salary reduction plan, known as a 401(k) plan. This operates similarly to an IRA, in that you set aside part of your salary. The amount is set by the company and the tax laws, but it can exceed the maximum required for IRAs. The amount set aside, and the earnings, are not taxable income until distributed. However, unlike IRAs, sometimes the employer may match your contribution. The money in your 401(k) plan is somewhat accessible in hardship situations. Also you can usually borrow from your 401(k) plan.

CHAPTER 11

Protecting Yourself Against Crime and Fraud

CRIME AND CONSUMER FRAUD CONTINUE TO BE A MAJOR CONCERN for retirees and other senior citizens as well as for the rest of the population. Seniors are more likely to be victims of crime because they are perceived to be easy marks by criminals. Whether you are at home, on the streets, or in your car, you can expect to encounter crime or fraud.

Each year there are more than 6 million burglaries; one every five seconds with reported losses of nearly $2 billion a year. A car is stolen every thirty seconds amounting to more than one-and-a-half-million cars a year at a value of nearly $8 billion. A recent wave of armed, sometimes fatal carjackings in the nation's suburbs, inner cities, and on the highways has raised fears that there are no safe havens from crime.

We have always regarded our homes as our castles—safe refuge from crime. Likewise, our cars have been viewed as reasonably safe against intrusions. However, recent crime statistics clearly show that our homes, cars, and even the streets, are not protected from criminal activity.

PROTECTING YOUR HOME

Statistics indicate that the typical burglar often lives in the neighborhood within a mile of the burglary. Although he is usually an amateur, he can easily break into most homes. The situation is likely to worsen unless you take some effective means to safeguard yourself and your home.

There are several practical crime fighting techniques you can implement to protect your home. You can start by inspecting all doors, windows, and other points of entry into your home. Your exterior doors should be solid core or metal and firmly attached to solid frames and to the house. All outside doors should have the hinges on the inside which are nonremovable. Those doors should also have deadbolt locks because these are difficult to pry or kick open. You should avoid having any breakable glass within three and one-half feet of the door locks. Use doors with unbreakable glass or which have a wide-angle peep hole to allow you to see visitors without having to open the door. If you have sliding doors, be sure that both panels are prevented from being lifted off the track. When the sliding doors are locked, use a rod to wedge the panels shut, in case the lock is picked or broken.

Securely lock your windows at night and when you are away from home. Consider putting shutters or metal grating on windows at ground level for added security. Also look at an alarm system for the windows and doors. Keep all trees and shrubs trimmed away from windows and doors so that they do not provide hidden cover for an intruder. Install good outdoor lighting at doors and windows. Motion sensitive lighting can be an inexpensive and effective crime-fighting technique.

If you are going away for an extended period, your house should appear as if someone is at home. Leave on an inside light and a radio. Have a neighbor keep an eye on your house and collect newspapers and mail. You can usually request that your post office and paper carrier hold your mail and newspapers until you return.

If you are a woman living alone, use only your first initials and your last name for your mailbox and telephone listing. Always verify the identity of repairmen, utility men, and other strangers before you let them into your home. Because senior citizens are greatly impacted by mail theft, you should consider having your paychecks, pension, and social security checks deposited directly into your bank account. Another crime deterrent is to mark your household items and other property to make them easier to trace.

Perhaps the most effective way to fight crime in your neighborhood is through a group of neighbors, organized as a community watch, helping each other. Through organization and communication with your neighbors, you can stop most crime in your community before it happens. And for those crimes you can't stop, you can help obtain convictions against criminals by thorough observations and testimony. Get to know the residents in your neighborhood and get involved in watching the activities on your block and in the community. Make a diagram showing every home in your immediate area and the names, addresses, and telephone numbers of the owners and residents. Tell them when you notice something unusual happening around their homes. Also report any suspicious behavior to the police.

Many people feel uncomfortable with firearms and are usually afraid to keep a gun around the house. Because of the alarming number of burglaries and other violent crimes, there may be situations where access to a gun at home can be advantageous. If you are comfortable and familiar with the use of a firearm, you may want to consider keeping a gun at home. There is plenty of merit in the philosophy for owning a gun that "it is better to have a gun and not need it, than to need one and not have it." If you own a gun, make sure that it is properly licensed and registered. Make sure that you handle and use it safely and keep it securely out of the reach of children.

PREVENTING CRIMES AGAINST YOU AND YOUR CAR

Auto thefts and carjackings over the past year have startled everyone. You must be proactive in safeguarding your car and yourself to combat these dreaded violations. Lock your doors and roll your windows up while driving to keep someone from entering your car. Keep your car in gear while waiting at traffic lights and stop signs and observe everything that is happening around you. Always keep enough distance from the car in front of you to allow room to move your car if needed. Conceal your purse, wallet, and other valuables from view, even while driving in your locked car.

Try to avoid travelling on dark, deserted streets. Although travelling on major streets and highways may take extra time, your life may depend on it. Refuse all hitchhikers a ride, no matter how harmless they appear. Monitor the frequent routes you travel and identify some safe, public spots where you can get emergency assistance if necessary. Make note of the location of police stations, fire stations, government offices, hospitals, service stations, convenience stores, churches, and other places you can go to for help.

If someone tries to accost you or follow you, keep your doors locked and your windows up, use your emergency flashers and horn, and drive quickly and carefully to a safe public place. Do not drive home as this will only let the follower know where you live. If your car is bumped on the road and you are not comfortable getting out, motion to the other driver and drive to the nearest police station or safe place.

If your car breaks down on the road, again, try to make it to a service station or one of your safe places. Otherwise, get off the road to avoid being hit by another vehicle. You may have to drive on a flat tire to do this, but the tire is replaceable and your life is not. Turn on your emergency flashers and place flares or other emergency signals you have conspicuously near the car. Place a white cloth or handkerchief on your antenna or door handle. Call for help if there is a telephone or motorist call box nearby. If not, get into your car, lock the doors and windows, and wait for help. If a stranger stops to help, remain in your locked car and ask the person to call the police or someone else for help. Likewise, if you see a motorist broken down on the highway, do not get out of your car because it could be a trap. Rather, get to a phone and call for help.

When parking your car, always leave it in a well-lit and well-travelled area. Check to make sure that you did not leave your keys in your car and that the doors are locked. Eighty percent of stolen cars are left unlocked and 40 percent have the keys left in the ignition. Do not leave spare keys hidden in your car. Hide all valuables from view. Consider using an antitheft device or alarm when your car is left unattended. When returning to your car, check carefully to make sure no one is hiding in your car before you get in. Exercise caution when returning home to be certain that there is no suspicious activity nearby. Blow your horn and have someone inside turn on lights or open the door for you.

It is not recommended that you carry a gun in your car or on your person, because it is generally prohibited in most states. However, you should consider carrying a canister of Mace or other attack repellant, or even a small knife. Don't be afraid to use these and other forms of self-defense in an attack, if you can do so without provoking harm to yourself. Retreating from an attacker and calling the police is always preferable to trying to conquer the attacker alone. Statistics indicate that you are less likely to suffer harm if you cooperate with an assailant rather than resisting. In any situation always try to remain calm and use common sense and caution.

Contact your local police for information on getting involved in or starting a neighborhood watch, self-defense techniques, and other crime prevention methods.

CONSUMER FRAUDS AGAINST SENIOR CITIZENS

Although consumer fraud is a major problem for all consumers, it has a harsher impact on senior citizens. It is important that you be a wise consumer and investor to protect yourself from becoming a victim of consumer fraud. The following discussion will help you to guard against the common crimes of consumer fraud against senior citizens. The U.S. Senate Special Committee on Aging has continually investigated the problem of consumer fraud against the elderly. The Committee found the following to be the ten most harmful frauds.

Medical Frauds

Not surprisingly, seniors are particularly concerned about their health. This concern creates a large vulnerability to quacks, miracle cures, hospital frauds, aging cures, medical aids, and other medical frauds of all kinds. Because seniors often forego proper medical care in response to the promises of these charlatans, and because of the genuine danger from contaminated compounds, the committee ranked medical frauds as the single most harmful fraud against the elderly.

Among the most frequent medical frauds are unproven remedies that promise relief, but are not supported by scientific evidence. Common examples are the various hair restorative compounds, cures for baldness, miracle diet programs, aging inhibitors, wrinkle reducers, sex aids, cure-alls, and pain relievers. Whatever the price, whatever the product, most of these cons sell hope—hope for the relief of pain, restoration of youth, and delay of death.

Home Repair and Improvement Frauds

Seventy-one percent of the elderly own their own homes. The majority of these homes were built before 1940. Only 11 percent of the houses where the household was headed by a senior were built since 1970. This combination of the number of elderly who own homes and the age of these dwellings is particularly attractive to phony repairmen. In fact, home repair and improvement frauds were found to be the most frequent frauds committed against the elderly.

Generally, phony home repairmen make a direct approach. They may appear at the victim's house posing as a city official or claim to have been referred by a neighbor down the street. Whatever the excuse, they quickly note some fundamental flaw in the house that must be repaired immediately. They specialize in roofing and siding, insulation, furnace repair, chimney replacements, wet basements, and driveway topping. Typically, they promise quick, efficient service at bargain rates, take a large downpayment, and never return.

Bunco Schemes

Bunco is a generic term of swindling schemes or confidence games. There are currently over eight hundred known bunco schemes. The three most common bunco schemes are summarized below.

- *The Pigeon Drop:* In the most common variation of this scheme, an older person is approached by strangers who claim to have found a large bag containing cash. Through a series of deceptions, the victim is convinced to put up "good faith" money to share in the find. The victim is asked to put the good faith money in a purse or parcel for safekeeping. In the final deception, the victim is distracted and the parcel containing his or her money is switched for another.
- *The Bank Examiner:* In this scheme, the con artist portrays himself as a good samaritan. He generally poses as a bank official and requests the assistance of the victim in checking on an employee suspected of defrauding the bank. Alternatively, the con may indicate there is reason to believe the victim's records are inaccurate and should be checked. Once the con has the victim's confidence, he persuades the victim to withdraw large sums from his or her bank account.
- *The Phony Official:* In these cons, the swindler poses as a representative of an official agency, such as Medicare, Social Security, the local zoning board, or some other agency. Once contact is made, the victim is persuaded that he or she needs insurance to cover medical costs not covered by Medicare, must repair his home, or replace appliances.

Insurance Frauds

The National Center for Health Services Research estimated in 1981 that 83.9 percent of the civilian, noninstitutionalized population had full-time, year-round insurance coverage. Those sixty-five and over—in part because of Medicare—showed year-round coverage rates of 97.8 percent. By contrast, young adults showed year-round coverage rates of 70 percent. These figures reflect seniors' concerns for the probability and effect of illness which makes them particularly susceptible to insurance frauds. The most flagrant of these abuses involve so-called Medigap insurance and cancer insurances.

Medigap policies are designed to cover the gaps in Medicare's coverage. Over 20 million of these policies have been sold to seniors at a cost of about $4 billion. Although most Medigap policies are legitimate, many are sold through fraudulent sales tactics to senior citizens who do not need them. Cancer insurance is among the hottest insurance sales items. There are currently over 20 million insurance policies in effect. So many questions have been raised with respect to these policies that they may be banned in some states.

The following techniques are often used by unscrupulous insurance agents:

- *Stacking* refers to the practice of persuading the victim to buy more policies than are needed.
- *Rolling-over* refers to the practice of attempting to persuade the victim to replace his existing policy with a "better" or "more comprehensive" one.
- *Misrepresentation* is a deliberate deception as to the policy's coverage.
- *Cleansheeting* refers to the agent's forgery of the victim's signature on a new policy.
- *Switching* refers to the type of fraud where the salesman switches policies so that the coverage obtained and the premium is different than the victim believed.

Social Frauds

Social frauds draw on a victim's charity, compassion, loneliness, and vanity. Charity frauds take advantage of the best instincts of people. The most frequent charity frauds involve bogus charities or religious groups, misrepresentation of association with a charity or religious group, and misrepresentation of the benefits or uses of contributions. Companionship clubs or "lonely hearts" clubs prey on the loneliness of their victims. Fear of growing old, becoming isolated and alone, are exploited with phony computer dating services, dancing lessons, or "dues" for social clubs.

Housing and Land Frauds

Land sales frauds cost U.S. citizens millions of dollars a year. Advertisements are designed to persuade the unwary to buy property they have never seen. All too frequently, the idyllic property in the brochure turns out to be swampland, or desert property far from the nearest town.

Similar misrepresentations are made with regard to vacation homes, time-sharing properties, and retirement homes. Often the buyer finds the romantic hide-away he purchased is without utility connections, or that the time-sharing resort sold more time than was available.

Business Opportunity and Investment Frauds

For retirees and others living on fixed incomes, business and investment frauds present a powerful attraction. For a relatively modest investment or through some irresistible business opportunity, the victim is offered the promise of great rewards. In one case, a Cleveland promoter sold jewelry franchises to 540 investors who responded to newspaper ads. The con collected $3.5 million with this scheme. All that the victims received for their investment was $100 worth of costume jewelry.

The other major variation—and one particularly targeted at the elderly—involves work-at-home schemes of all kinds. Some of the more common work-at-home schemes include worm farms, envelope addressing, envelope stuffing, and sew-at-home schemes. One sew-at-home scheme drew 200,000 applicants who were allowed, for a small registration fee, to take a sewing test to see if they qualified for employment. Not surprisingly, no one qualified and no refunds were given.

Nursing Home Frauds

About 1.2 million seniors live in the nation's 25,000 nursing homes. They constitute about 90 percent of all nursing home residents. Further, the probability of being institutionalized increases with age, from one out of a hundred in the age group of sixty-five to seventy-four to one out of five of those over eighty-five years old. Abuses in nursing homes have been well publicized during the last decade, largely due to the efforts of the Senate Special Committee on Aging. Most of the concern that has been generated has focused on the quality of care issues and indications of Medicare and Medicaid fraud. Because the government, as the purchaser of services, is so evidently defrauded by these activities, we have often lost sight of the fact that the seniors are often also defrauded. They may be conned into paying an "admission fee" to purchase a place in a Medicaid facility, overcharged for specific services, defrauded out of personal maintenance funds, and forced to pay for specific services and supplies that should be included in the home's per diem rate.

One of the more recent variations on this theme is the development of "lifecare" facilities. In these instances, seniors are persuaded to sign over all of their assets with the promise that they will be taken care of until they die. Often, the facility changes ownership or goes out of business, leaving the seniors stranded and exposed.

While there are federal and state criminal and civil laws to protect against these frauds, people are still falling prey to the frauds every day. Some swindlers are caught and go to jail or pay fines and restitution, but there are always others to take their place. The greatest weapon to protect yourself against them is consumer education. To be forewarned is to be forearmed. That gives potential victims more protection than any book full of laws.

SOURCES OF HELP FOR CONSUMERS

There are many resources available to you to assist you with consumer problems and inquiries. These include your Better Business Bureaus, state and local consumer agencies, local newspapers, radio and television stations, state attorney general's office, and state department on aging. Also available are federal agencies, trade associations, and consumer groups. Look in your telephone directory or visit your local library for the complete names, addresses, and telephone numbers for these organizations.

You can receive a free copy of the *Consumer's Resource Handbook* by writing to the Consumer Information Center, Pueblo, CO 81009. This booklet provides a listing of federal, state, and local government agencies, and private businesses and organizations that can help you as a consumer. The U.S. Office of Consumer Affairs, Washington, DC 20233 compiles a consumer's resource handbook which provides useful information on how to be a smart consumer. Some other sources of assistance are as follows:

- For mail order and door-to-door sales inquiries contact: Federal Trade Commission, Correspondence Branch, Washington, DC 20580
- For mail order sales inquiries contact: U.S. Postal Service, Chief Postal Inspector, Room 3517, Washington, DC 20260; (202) 245-5445
- For complaints and information about mail order sales, write: Director, Mail Order Action Line Service, Direct Marketing Association, 6 East 43rd Street, New York, NY 10017; (212) 689-4977
- For complaints and information about door-to-door sales, write: Code Administrator, Direct Selling Association, 1730 M Street, N.W., Suite 60, Washington, DC 20036

Other associations you can contact about specific products or services are listed in directories of trade associations at your local library. You can also contact consumer groups such as the following:

- American Association of Retired Persons, 1909 K Street, N.W., Washington, DC 20049
- Consumer Federation of America, 1424 P Street, N.W., Suite 604, Washington, DC 20036

Other consumer groups are listed in guides at your local library. Directories of businesses and their addresses can be found there as well. Many directories give the address of top officers, public relations departments, and customer service sections.

CHAPTER 12

UNDERSTANDING TAXES DURING RETIREMENT

IN GENERAL, THE FEDERAL INCOME TAX LAWS APPLY EQUALLY TO ALL taxpayers regardless of age. However, certain provisions give special treatment to older Americans. Specific tax benefits are available to older Americans and are listed here.

- Taxpayers sixty-five or older benefit from a higher gross income threshold for filing a federal income tax return. File Form 1040 or 1040A to get this benefit. (You are considered sixty-five on the day before your sixty-fifth birthday.)
- Taxpayers who qualify and who meet the age requirements may benefit from the following:
    - Credit for the elderly or the disabled
    - Exclusion of gain on the sale of their home
    - Increased standard deduction

HOW TO GET TAX INFORMATION

The Internal Revenue Service (IRS) and the U.S. Senate Special Committee on Aging have compiled a variety of publications to assist older Americans in preparing their federal income tax returns.

Much of the information in this chapter is drawn from these publications and further explained to assure that you claim every legitimate income tax credit, exemption, and deduction due you as a senior taxpayer. Keep in mind that the tax laws are constantly changing and you need to keep informed of changes that may impact you as a senior citizen. For complex tax issues you may need the assistance of a knowledgeable tax attorney or accountant.

The IRS has prepared many free publications to help answer your tax questions. In addition to the general publication 17, *Your Federal Income Tax,* publications are available on specific topics, such as:

1 *Your Rights as a Taxpayer*
505 *Tax Withholding and Estimated Tax*
524 *Credit for the Elderly or the Disabled*
525 *Taxable and Nontaxable Income*
530 *Tax Information for Homeowners*
554 *Tax Information for Older Americans*
575 *Pension and Annuity Income (Including Simplified General Rule)*
596 *Earned Income Credit*
721 *Comprehensive Tax Guide to U.S. Civil Service Retirement Benefits*
907 *Tax Information for Persons with Handicaps or Disabilities*
910 *Guide to Free Tax Services*
915 *Social Security Benefits and Equivalent Railroad Retirement Benefits*

Any IRS publication can be ordered by mail, using the order form in your tax package or by calling the IRS toll free at 1-800-829-3676. They also may be found at public libraries, post offices, and some banks.

There are other special IRS programs offering free assistance to you. Through the Tax Counseling for the Elderly (TCE) program, IRS-trained volunteers assist individuals age sixty or older with their tax returns at neighborhood locations in many areas. In addition, certain Volunteer Income Tax Assistance (VITA) aides have been trained to help older Americans with their tax returns.

YOUR FILING STATUS

In general, your filing status depends on whether you are considered single or married on the last day of your tax year. If you file a calendar-year return, your last day generally is December 31. Each filing status has a different tax rate. If more than one filing status applies to you, choose the one that gives you the lowest tax. Each of the five filing statuses are explained below:

1. *Single:* Generally, you are considered single if you were never married or you were divorced as of December 31 of the tax year. You are also considered single if you were legally separated, according to your state law, under a decree of divorce or a decree of separate maintenance.
2. *Married filing a joint return:* Generally, you are married if you were legally married as of December 31, even if you did not live with your spouse during the tax year. You are also considered married if your spouse died in the tax year and you did not remarry in that year. You may file a joint return even if only one spouse had all the income.
3. *Married filing a separate return:* If you are married, you can choose to file separate tax returns. After the due date of the return, however, you may not choose to file separate returns if you first filed a joint return for that year. You must provide your spouse's full name and Social Security number in the box provided for it on your tax return. Generally, you report only your own income, exemptions, deductions, and credits.
4. *Head of household:* If you were unmarried or considered unmarried as of December 31 of the tax year, and you provide more than half the cost of keeping up a home (that was the main home) for yourself and your unmarried child (regardless of his/her age or whether he/she was financially dependent on you) for more than six months, you may be eligible to file

as head of household. You may also be able to file as head of household if you are entitled to claim other relatives such as your mother or father, or your married child as dependents.

5. *Qualifying widow(er) with dependent child:* If your spouse died and you remained unmarried during the tax year, you may be able to continue to pay taxes at the lower joint tax rates if you satisfy all of the following:
   - Your dependent child lived with you for the entire year, except for temporary absences
   - You paid more than one-half of the cost of keeping up your home
   - You were entitled to file a joint return with your spouse for the year your spouse died

Do You Have to File a Tax Return?

The tax laws and regulations specify who must file a federal tax return based on gross income and filing status. The filing deadline is April 15 of the year following the tax year, unless you request an extension by the April 15 date. Tax returns which are postmarked after April 15 may be subject to penalties and interest.

The filing requirements based on filing status and gross income for the tax year 1997 are given below:

FILING STATUS	GROSS INCOME
Single	
Under age 65	over $6,800
Age 65 or older	over $7,850
Married Filing Joint Return	
Both spouses under age 65	over $12,200
One spouse age 65 or older	over $13,000
Both spouses age 65 or older	over $13,800
Not living with spouse at the end of year (or on date spouse died)	over $2,650
Married Filing Separate Return	over $2,650

Head of Household

Under age 65 .... over $8,700

Age 65 or older .... over $9,700

Qualifying Widow(er)

Under age 65 .... over $9,550

Age 65 or older .... over $10,350

If you were self-employed and your net earnings were at least $400, then you must file a return to pay Social Security and Medicare taxes. This rule applies regardless of your age, whether or not you are receiving Social Security benefits, and even if you do not otherwise have to file a federal tax return. You are self-employed if you carry on a trade or business as a sole proprietor, a member of a partnership, or an independent contractor. This includes certain part-time work that you do at home or in addition to your regular job.

Even if you are not required to file a tax return, you should do so if you want to claim a refund for any taxes withheld. You should also file to get a refund of the earned income credit if you are eligible for the credit. If you do not file, you will not get a refund.

Claiming Exemptions and Dependents

You are allowed a deduction for each exemption that you claim on your tax return. The personal exemption amount for tax year 1997 was $2,650. You can claim yourself, your spouse, your minor children, or any other relative or member of your household, if all five dependency tests are met for that individual. The amount of your exemption will be reduced or phased out beginning at an adjusted gross income of $90,900 (married filing separately), $121,200 (single), and $181,800 (married filing jointly).

There are five tests to determine whether someone is your dependent: relationship, married person, citizen or resident, income, and support tests. Each dependent must meet all five of the following tests.

1. *Relationship:* Your dependent must be either your relative or someone who lived in your home as a member of your household all year. Any relationships established by marriage are not treated as ended by divorce or death. The relationship must not violate local law.

   The following are considered your relatives:

   - Your child. Your child includes your son, daughter, step-child, adopted child, a child who lived in your home as a family member (if placed with you by an authorized placement agency for legal adoption), and a foster child (any child who lived in your home as a family member the whole year).
   - Your grandchild, great-grandchild, etc.
   - Your son-in-law, daughter-in-law
   - Your parent, grandparent, stepparent, parent-in-law
   - Your brother, sister, stepbrother, stepsister, brother-in-law, sister-in-law, half-brother, half-sister
   - If related by blood, your aunt, uncle, nephew, niece
2. *Married person:* Your married dependent cannot file a joint return. However, if neither the dependent nor the dependent's spouse is required to file, but they file a joint return to get a refund of all taxes withheld, you may claim the dependent if the other four tests are met.
3. *Citizen or resident:* The dependent must be either a U.S. citizen or resident alien, or a resident of Canada or Mexico, or your adopted child who is not a U.S. citizen but who lived with you all year in a foreign country.
4. *Income:* Generally, the dependent's gross income must be less than the prescribed amount. Gross income does not include nontaxable income, such as welfare benefits or nontaxable Social Security benefits. If your dependent was permanently and totally disabled and had income from services performed at a sheltered workshop school, that income is generally not included for purposes of the income test.

Your dependent child does not have to meet this income test if he or she was either under nineteen at the end of the tax year, or under age twenty-four at the end of the tax year and qualifies as a student.

5. *Support:* The general rule is that you must have provided over half the dependent's support during the tax year. If you file a joint return, support could come from either spouse. Support includes food, a place to live, clothing, medical and dental care, and education. Support also includes such items as a car and furniture, but only if they are given to the dependent solely for his or her own use or benefit. In figuring total support, use the actual cost of these items. However, you should figure the cost of a place to live at its fair rental value. In figuring support, you must include money used by the dependent for his or her own support, even if this money was not taxable. Examples are Social Security and welfare benefits, gifts, and savings. Support does not include such items as income tax, Social Security and Medicare taxes, life insurance premiums, scholarship and fellowship grants, or funeral expenses.

WHAT IS TAXABLE INCOME?

Generally, you must include in gross income everything you receive in payment for personal services, interest, dividends, rents, royalties, gain from the sale of property, and income from partnerships and other businesses. In addition to wages, salaries, commissions, tips, and fees, this includes other forms of compensation, such as fringe benefits and stock options.

You must report income in the form of goods or services at the fair market value of the goods or services you received. Income of particular interest to older Americans includes interest, dividends, gain from the sale of a main home, pensions and annuities, distributions from IRAs, and Social Security benefits.

Interest and Dividends

You must report all your taxable interest income. Interest earned on notes or bonds issued by a state or local government may not be taxable. You must show on your tax return any tax-exempt interest you received or accrued during the tax year. This is an information-reporting requirement and does not convert tax-exempt interest to taxable interest. Each payer of interest should send you a Form 1099-INT or a Form 1099-OID. A copy of the form is also sent to the IRS. Be sure to provide the payer of interest with your correct Social Security number and include all of this income on your return.

Dividends are distributions of money, stock, or other property that corporations pay to shareholders. You must report all your ordinary dividends. Each payer of dividends should send you a Form 1099-DIV. A copy of the form is also sent to the IRS. Be sure to provide the payer of dividends with your correct Social Security number and include all of the taxable income on your return. For more information on dividends and interest income, see IRS Publication 550.

Sale of Your Main Home

If you sold your main home during the year, you must report the sale or exchange of your home on Form 2110, "Sale of Your Home." For a home sale after May 6, 1997 you may be able to exclude up to $250,000 (for individuals) and $500,000 (for married couples) of gain from the sale of your home. Prior to this date, you were able to either postpone paying tax on some or all of the gain (if you bought a new home within two years) or to exclude up to $125,000 of the gain from your taxable income (if you were age fifty-five or older and met other requirements). You cannot deduct a loss on the sale of your home. The loss has no effect on the basis of your new home.

To qualify for full $250,000 or $500,000 exclusion, you must have owned and used the property sold as your principal residence for periods totalling two years or more during the five-year period ending on the date of the sale. For a married couple filing a joint return, either you or your spouse must meet the ownership requirement and both of you must meet the use requirement with respect to the home to qualify for the full $500,000 exclusion. Note that the exclusion typically does not apply if there has been a previous home sale or exchange for which the exclusion applied within the immediate prior two years.

For more complete information, get IRS Publication 523, *Tax Information for Selling Your Home.*

Pensions and Annuities

You should receive a Form 1099-R showing the amount of your pension or annuity. Your pension or annuity payments are fully taxable if you did not contribute to the cost of your pension or annuity. Fully taxable pensions and annuities also include military retirement pay shown on form 1099R and any taxable Railroad Retirement benefits shown in Form RRB-1099-R. If you contributed to your pension or annuity, then payments are not taxable up the amount of your contribution.

If your pension or annuity is not fully taxable and your Form 1099-R does not show the taxable part, you must use the General Rule to figure the taxable part. The General Rule is explained in Publication 939, *Pension General Rule (Nonsimplified Method).* But, if your annuity starting date was after July 1, 1986, you may be able to use the Simplified General Rule as explained in Publication 575, *Pension and Annuity Income (Including Simplified General Rule).* You are required to use the Simplified General Rule for annuities starting after November 18, 1996. If your pension is civil service, you should get Publication 721, *Comprehensive Tax Guide to U.S. Civil Service Retirement Benefits.*

If you receive a lump sum payment, you may be eligible to lower the taxes due on it by using Form 4972, *Tax on Lump-Sum Distributions.*

Distributions From Individual Retirement Arrangements (IRAs)

Distributions from an IRA, whether from principal or earnings, are generally fully taxable when received. See Publication 590, *Individual Retirement Arrangements (IRAs)*, for exceptions to this general rule, including rollovers and timely withdrawals of excess contributions. If you made nondeductible contributions to your IRA, you may have a cost basis in your IRA. The part representing a return of your nondeductible contributions is not taxed when distributed to you. A 10-percent tax in addition to the regular income tax applied to any distributions before age fifty-nine-and-one-half, except in certain cases such as the death or disability of the IRA owner or to pay for medical expenses.

You must withdraw the entire balance in your IRA or begin distributions by April 1 of the calendar year following the year in which you become age seventy-and-one-half to avoid substantial additional taxes. The required minimum distributions of any year after you turn seventy-and-one-half must be made by December 31 of that year. These distributions are taxable in the year received.

Social Security and Railroad Retirement

Generally, you will owe taxes on some (either 50 or 85 percent) of your Social Security and equivalent Railroad Retirement benefits if your total income (including half of your benefits) exceeds $25,000 for single and married persons (who live apart all year) filing a separate return, or $32,000 for married couples who file a joint return.

You should receive Form SSA-1099, Social Security Benefit Statement, if you received benefits in the tax year. This form will show any deductions made by Social Security from your total benefits, such as Medicare premiums, repayments of prior-year overpayments, etc. If you do not receive an SSA-1099 by early February or you believe the statement to be incorrect, you should call the SSA toll-free number, 1-800-234-5722.

To determine whether you must include any of your Social Security benefits in taxable income, add up your income from all sources including any tax-exempt interest you may have received and one-half of your net benefits. If your total income is $25,000 or less and you are a single person, or a married person filing separately and did not live with your spouse at any time during the year ($32,000 for married couples filing a joint return), then none of your benefits will be included. If your total income exceeds $25,000 and you are a single person or a married person filing separately and did not live with your spouse at any time during the year ($32,000 for married couples filing a joint return), then some of your benefits will be included. You will need to figure the taxable part of your benefits.

For more information, get Publication 915, *Social Security Benefits and Equivalent Railroad Retirement Benefits.*

NONTAXABLE INCOME

Under the tax laws certain items are exempt from income tax. Generally gifts and inheritances you receive are not taxable to you; the person making the gift/bequest already paid taxes, if any, on the income used to purchase the gift or to build the estate. However, if you later receive income such as interest, dividends, or rents from such property, that income is taxable to you. Department of Veterans Affairs (VA) payments and/or insurance proceeds paid at the death of the insured are usually tax free. Sickness and injury benefits, such as worker's compensation and disability payments, and public assistance payments are not taxable.

ADJUSTMENTS TO YOUR INCOME

Once you have figured your total income, you may "adjust" it downward with any of six major adjustments to arrive at adjusted gross income. You do not have to itemize to take these adjustments to income. Employee business expenses are no longer an adjustment to income (but they are an itemized deduction on Schedule A) except for certain performing artists and handicapped employees.

Individual Retirement Arrangements

You may be able to deduct contributions you make to an IRA in whole, or in part, depending on your circumstances. Earnings and gains on your IRA generally are not taxed until they are distributed to you. Generally, you can contribute up to $2,000 to an IRA. If you (or your spouse) were covered at any time during the year by an employer's retirement plan, your deduction may be limited. If your deduction is limited, you can still make nondeductible contributions up to your remaining contribution limit. If you file a joint return with your spouse (who did not work during the year), you may be eligible to contribute up to $2,250 into two separate IRAs (one for you and one for your spouse, a spousal IRA). You can divide the contribution between the two accounts in any way except that neither account can be credited with more than $2,000. See Publication 590 for more information. If you were age seventy-and-one-half or older by the end of the tax year, you cannot deduct any contributions made to your IRA or treat them as nondeductible contributions.

Keogh Plans

You must have net earnings from self-employment to claim a deduction for payments to a Keogh (H.R. 10) plan. For information on Keogh plans, see Publication 560, *Retirement Plans for the Self-Employed.*

One-Half of Self-Employment Tax

If you had income from self-employment and you owe self-employment tax, you may deduct one-half of that tax. But you will first need to complete Schedule SE to figure your deduction.

Other Adjustments to Income

In addition, you may be eligible to take certain other adjustments to income. These include self-employed health insurance, penalty on early withdrawal of savings, alimony paid, and jury duty pay given to your employers.

The Standard Deduction

The standard deduction reduced the need for many taxpayers to itemize their deductions. The standard deduction, which depends on your filing status (explained earlier) and whether you are sixty-five or older or blind, is figured separately. Once you have figured your standard deduction amount, you should then decide which gives you a higher tax benefit—taking the standard deduction or itemizing your deductions on Schedule A of Form 1040.

If you are age sixty-five or older or blind in the tax year, you are entitled to a higher standard deduction amount than taxpayers under sixty-five and not blind. If you are totally blind, attach a statement to this effect to your return. If you are partially blind, you must submit with your return each year a certified statement from an eye physician or registered optometrist.

For the 1997 tax year, the standard deduction was $4,150 for single taxpayers; $3,450 for married filing separate taxpayers; $6,050 for head-of-household taxpayers; and $6,900 for qualifying widows and widowers, and married-filing-jointly taxpayers. For taxpayers age sixty-five or older the standard deduction for the above taxpayers is $5,150, $4,250, $7,050, and $7,700, respectively.

Itemized Deductions

If your itemized deductions total more than your standard deduction, it will usually save you taxes to itemize. Use Schedule A (Form 1040) to itemize your deductions. These deductions can include the following:

Medical and Dental Expenses

Medical and dental expenses are payments you make for the diagnosis, treatment, or prevention of disease. They also include payments for treatment affecting any part or function of the body. Expenses for transportation to get medical care are included in medical expenses. Payments for insurance (including Medicare premiums) that provides medical care for you, your spouse, and dependents are included in medical expenses. Unreimbursed expenses are deductible when they exceed 7.5 percent of your adjusted gross income. Expenses may be deducted only in the year you paid them. If you charge medical expenses on your credit card, deduct the expenses in the year the charge is made.

Taxes

Deductions can be taken on any real estate, personal property, and state, local, or foreign income taxes you paid during the tax year.

Home Mortgage Interest

Generally, home mortgage interest is any interest you pay on a loan secured by your home (main home or a second home). These loans include (1) a mortgage to buy your home, (2) a second mortgage, (3) a line of credit, and (4) a home equity loan. In most cases, you will be able to deduct all of your home mortgage interest. Whether it is all deductible depends on the date you took out the mortgage, the amount of the mortgage, and your use of its proceeds. Get Publication 936 for more information on home mortgage interest.

Beginning in 1991, you can no longer deduct personal interest. Personal interest is any that is not home mortgage interest, investment interest, or business interest. Personal interest includes interest you pay on car loans, installment purchases, credit cards, and personal loans.

Charitable Contributions

A charitable contribution is a contribution or gift to, or for the use of, a qualified organization. Any organization can tell you if it is a qualified organization. To deduct your contributions, you must make them in cash or other property before the end of your tax year.

Casualty or Theft Losses

You may deduct casualty losses, such as those that result from a tornado, flood, storm, fire, or auto accident (provided it was not caused by a willful act or willful negligence), or theft losses. Your casualty loss deduction is generally the lesser of (1) the decrease in fair market value of the property as a result of the casualty or theft, or (2) your adjusted basis in the property before the casualty or theft. This amount must be reduced by any insurance or other reimbursement you receive.

Your nonbusiness casualty or theft losses are deductible only to the extent that your total losses during the year exceed 10 percent of your adjusted gross income after reducing each separate casualty or theft by $100. You must use Form 4684 to figure your casualty or theft loss.

You may not deduct a casualty or theft loss that is covered by insurance unless you filed a timely insurance claim for reimbursement. However, even if you did not file an insurance claim, you may deduct the part of the loss not covered by insurance. For more information, see Publication 547, *Nonbusiness Disasters, Casualties, and Thefts.*

Miscellaneous Deductions

Miscellaneous deductions (such as professional dues, educational expenses, uniforms, and other expenses) can be taken to the extent that they exceed 2 percent of your adjusted gross income. For more information, see Publication 529.

TAX CREDITS

Tax credits are beneficial because they directly reduce the tax you owe. You can generally take a credit for child- and dependent-care expenses, if you paid someone to care for your disabled spouse, disabled dependent, or child under age thirteen so you could work or look for work. See Publication 503 for more information on the *Child and Dependent Care Credit.*

You may be able to claim the credit for the elderly and the disabled if you are (1) age sixty-five or over, or (2) under age sixty-five and retired on a permanent and total disability for which you received taxable disability benefits in the tax year. See Publication

524 if you want more information on the *Credit for the Elderly or the Disabled.*

The Earned Income Credit may be available to you if you have a qualifying child living with you and meet certain earnings and income requirements. See Publication 596 for more information on the *Earned Income Credit.*

ESTATE AND GIFT TAXES

You generally do not have to pay tax on any cash or property you receive as a gift or inheritance. Likewise, any gift or inheritance you pass on is generally tax free to the recipient. If you make a gift of more than $10,000 ($20,000 for married couples) to any one individual in the same year, you—but not the recipient—may be required to pay a gift tax. Remember, no taxes are paid on gifts between spouses, regardless of the amount, and no federal estate tax, nor any estate tax return, is due on an inheritance if the value of the decedent's gross estate is $625,000 or less.

For more information, get Publication 448, *Federal Estate and Gift Taxes.*

CHAPTER 13

ENJOYING VACATIONS AT HOME AND ABROAD

WHETHER YOU RETIRE AT AGE FIFTY-FIVE OR SIXTY-FIVE THE ODDS are that you have probably put off travelling to some parts of the United States or the world until that time many call the "golden years." Even if you have not yet reached your golden years, the fact that your children are on their own provides more freedom to give into that urge to "see some of the world before I die."

Travel can be immensely rewarding and fun. Yet, we all know people whose well-thought-out vacation turned into a nightmare because of accommodations that were less than optimal or whose vacation was overcome by unexpected events. This chapter includes some general advice on vacations and foreign travel as a way of helping you insure that your trip is pleasurable and carefree. Most would agree that a little forethought can go a long way towards positioning yourself to recover financially and emotionally should some unforeseen events ruin your vacation, or to avoid these problems in the first place.

PLANNING FOR YOUR VACATION

There is a lot you can do to prepare for your trip. The first thing is to learn something about the places or countries you plan to visit. There are several good sources of information such as:

- Travel agents who can provide brochures and tourist information
- Local bookstores and public libraries
- Tourist information offices located in many large cities
- Airlines which may also have maps and brochures on the countries they serve
- Foreign embassies or consulates in many major cities (Look for their addresses in your local telephone directory or in the library)

The next step is to make travel, lodging, and other necessary arrangements for your vacation. Although you can try to handle these arrangements yourself, it is usually more expedient and more relaxing to deal with a reputable travel agent. Most trips and vacations you take will involve arrangements for services and accommodations that you simply can not inspect before paying for them. Also, it may not be easy for you to evaluate and compare travel and vacation options without the assistance of an experienced travel agent.

Planning a good vacation takes time. Be sure to allow yourself and your travel agent enough time to make reservations, submit payments, and receive any necessary tickets, vouchers, or other documents. Talk to your travel agent as early as possible to begin making plans. Let the agent know what you plan to spend and what your expectations are.

With over 20,000 members in 125 countries, the American Society of Travel Agents (ASTA) is the oldest and perhaps the most influential travel trade association in the world. ASTA includes travel agencies, airlines, hotels, railroads, cruise lines, tour operators, car rental companies, and travel schools. Because these travel agents are required to adhere to a code of ethics, you should consider using ASTA agents, or members of similar travel industry trade groups. For further information on ASTA and participating members contact: American Society of Travel Agents, Inc., 1101 King Street, Alexandria, VA 22314; (703) 739-2782.

Selecting a Packaged Tour

Unless your are visiting relatives, a packaged tour may be the solution to organizing a vacation. Here are some basic guidelines for selecting a reliable tour program and for choosing the right tour for you.

These days packaged tours come in many different "flavors," despite their image of being overly regimented and lacking in adventure or sophistication. Now you can select vacations that range from the most meticulously preplanned escorted tour to the free-wheeling spontaneity of a fly/drive holiday. Overall, package tours are appealing because they offer greater savings and the peace of mind that comes from knowing that your vacation was planned by professionals.

One good thing to look for initially is whether your tour company is a member of the United States Tours Operators Association (USTOA). According to the association's code, the member's brochures must be clear and accurate. Membership requires companies to have been in business at least three years, carry a minimum of $1 million professional liability insurance, and participate in the association's $5 Million Consumer Protection Plan. This plan protects you against financial loss resulting from bankruptcy or insolvency of active tour operators. Usually when you see the USTOA symbol in a tour brochure, it is meant to be your assurance of good value for your money, reliability, and integrity in tourism.

When choosing a tour, the most important step is to decide what kind of travel operator will provide the experience and services that you want. When reading a tour brochure, be sure you understand what is and what is not included. It's what you don't know and don't expect that can be irritating and disappointing during your trip. Always pay close attention to the price quoted. For example, is the price all inclusive or is it for the land arrangements only? Several other factors may add to the tour price, such as optional excursions, service charges, taxes, weekend air surcharges, and peak season supplements.

Pay attention to the day-to-day itineraries featured in most tour brochures because they are a guide to what you can expect to see and do on the tour. If you are considering an escorted tour, distinguish between the cities and sites that you will simply be driving through and those you will be spending time in. Make sure you are comfortable with the amount of time spent at each location, or the amount of time spent on a bus or walking. Also, is there enough free time for shopping and other activities you want to do? When it comes to sleeping arrangements note the descriptions and ratings of the hotel featured. Keep in mind that hotel rating in other countries may not always reflect American standards. In other words, a "deluxe" hotel in one country could differ in size, style, and degree of luxury from a similarly rated hotel in another country.

Be sure to look for the section of the brochure outlining the "conditions." This very important section usually covers details about reservations, cancellations, refunds, and availability of insurance. Other items typically covered include meals, accommodations, air transportation, sight-seeing, baggage allowance, health information, and things not included in the tour price. Go over this information carefully before reaching a decision.

Before selecting a tour operator you should find out how long the company has been in business under the same ownership, and if it was recently merged or sold, who and how experienced are the new owners. Also, how long have they been operating tours to your area of interest? You should consider purchasing default insurance that will pay if your tour operator does not perform.

TRAVELLING BY AIR

Newspapers, radio, and television advertise discount and special-rate airline tickets almost every day. The variety of air service available ranges from super-premium service where a limousine picks you up at your door, to no-frills, low-cost service where you carry your own bags.

Your travel agent is a good source of information about air fares, schedules, baggage limits, and other features. In addition, travel agencies can sometimes obtain discount tickets to popular destinations. Check with your travel agent, even if the airlines are sold out. You may have to be flexible in your travel plans in order to get the lowest fare. There may be complicated conditions you have to meet to qualify for a discount.

When making airline travel arrangements, always ask about fees or penalties for changing or canceling your reservation. Find out if there is a cut-off date for making and changing reservations without having to pay more. Some airlines will not increase the price of your ticket after it has been issued and paid for. However, simply holding a reservation without a ticket does not guarantee the ticket price. Other airlines may reserve the right to increase your ticket price anytime before your departure. Be sure to find out which price increase policy applies to your tickets.

Your airline ticket will show the flight numbers, dates and departure times, and the status of your reservation. If the "status" box is marked "OK," this means that you are confirmed. Otherwise your reservation is not certain and you may only be wait-listed. You should reconfirm your reservation before you start your trip. Oftentimes airline flight schedules will change. On international flights, most airlines require that you reconfirm your departure and return reservations at least seventy-two hours before each flight or your reservation may be canceled. Airlines do not guarantee their flight schedules because many things can go wrong, such as bad weather, air traffic delays, and mechanical problems. If your flight is canceled, some airlines will reschedule you on the first available flight to your destination at no additional charge.

Most airlines overbook their flights and some passengers are "bumped." If you are bumped involuntarily, you are generally entitled to be compensated. The amount depends on the price of your ticket and the length of time you are delayed. If you are bumped involuntarily and the airline arranges substitute transportation that is scheduled to get you to your destination (including later connections) within one hour of your original scheduled arrival time, there is no compensation. If the airline arranges substitute transportation that is scheduled to arrive at your destination more than one hour but less than two hours (four hours on international flights) after your original arrival time, the airline must pay you an amount equal to the one-way fare to your final destination, with a $200 maximum. If the substitute transportation is scheduled to get you to your destination more than two hours later (four hours internationally), or if the airline does not make any substitute travel arrangements for you, the compensation doubles (200 percent of the fare, $200 maximum). You always get to keep your original ticket, and you can use it on another flight or have it refunded. The denied boarding compensation is essentially a payment for your inconvenience.

To qualify for compensation for being bumped, you must have a confirmed reservation, meet the ticketing or check-in deadline, and be departing from some place within the United States. No compensation is due to you for scheduled flights of sixty or less passengers, flights where a smaller plane is substituted for the original one, or flights that are chartered.

At check-in, the airline will put baggage destination tags on your luggage and give you the stubs to use as claim checks. Each tag has a three-letter code and flight number that show the baggage sorters on which place and to which airport your luggage is supposed to go. Double-check the tag and flight number before your bags go down the conveyor belt. Also, make sure that you have put your name and address on each of your bags. Be sure all of the tabs from previous trips are removed from your bags, since they may confuse busy baggage handlers. Don't lose your claim checks—they are your only proof that you really did check bags with the airline.

If your suitcase arrives smashed or torn, the airline will usually pay for repairs. If it cannot be fixed, they will negotiate a settlement to pay you its depreciated value. The same holds true for clothing packed inside. Report external damage in writing before you leave the airport. If your bags are delayed, lost, or damaged on a domestic flight, the airline may invoke a $1,250 ceiling on the amount of money they will pay you. When your luggage and its contents are worth more than that, you may want to purchase "excess valuation," if available, from the airline as you check in. This will increase the carrier's potential liability. The airline may refuse to sell excess valuation on some items that are especially valuable or breakable, such as antiques, musical instruments, jewelry, manuscripts, negotiable securities, and cash.

On international trips, the liability limits are set by a treaty called the Warsaw Convention. Unless you buy excess valuation, the liability limit is 250 French gold francs for each kilo (a kilo is equal to about 2.2 pounds) of checked baggage, and the airlines have a formula for converting this limit into U.S. dollars. The disclosure statement on the back of your ticket explains your rights and responsibilities. However, some airlines do not put all of the contract terms on the ticket, but may elect to incorporate terms by reference into a separate contract of carriage which you can inspect or request a copy of.

Travelling Outside the United States

If you are planning a trip outside of the United States, you should check for travel advisories before finalizing your destination. The U.S. State Department issues travel advisories to alert U.S. citizens to conditions overseas that may affect them adversely. Three types of travel advisories you are likely to encounter are as follows:

- Warning recommends deferral of travel to all or part of a country

- Caution advises about unusual security conditions, including the potential for unexpected detention, unstable political conditions, or serious health problems. It is not intended to deter travel to a country.
- Notice provides information on situations that do not present a broad-scale risk, but which could result in inconvenience or difficulty for Americans travelling abroad.

Travel advisories are posted at U.S. passport agencies and are distributed to the travel and airline industry.

Travel document requirements vary from country to country but for most you will need a passport or other proof of citizenship, plus a visa or a tourist card. You may also need evidence that you have enough money for your trip and have ongoing or return transportation tickets. All U.S. citizens need a passport to depart or enter the United States. The only exceptions are short-term travel between the U.S. and Mexico, Canada, and some countries in the Caribbean. Even if you are not required to have a passport to visit a country, U.S. Immigration requires you to prove your U.S. citizenship and identity when you reenter the United States. Make certain that you take adequate documentation to pass through U.S. Immigration upon your return. A passport is best, but other documents useful to prove citizenship include a certified copy of your birth certificate, a certificate of naturalization, a certificate of citizenship, or a report of birth abroad of a citizen of the United States. To prove your identity either a valid driver's license or a government identification card that includes a photo or a physical description is typically adequate. If you already have a passport please pay attention to the expiration date. Certain countries will not permit you to enter and will not give you a visa if the remaining validity is less than six months. And if you return to the United States with an expired passport, you are subject to a passport waiver fee of $100 at the port of entry.

All persons must have their own passport, so family members are not permitted to be included in each others' passports. For your first passport, you must appear in person with a completed form at a U.S. passport agency, federal or state court, or post office authorized to accept passport applications. You should be able to find the addresses of passport acceptance facilities in your area in the government listings of your local telephone book. Since the flow of applications and the necessary processing time is unpredictable, you should apply for your passport several months in advance of your planned departure. Passport agencies may, however, expedite issuance in cases of genuine documented emergencies.

Be sure to safeguard your passport. Its loss could cause you unnecessary travel complications as well as significant expense. Just in case you have to replace it, photocopy the date page of your passport and keep it in a separate place from your valuables. In addition, leave the passport number, date, and place of issuance with a relative or friend in the United States.

In many cases you will need a visa from a country you plan to visit. A visa is an endorsement or stamp placed in your passport by a foreign government that permits you to visit that country for a specified purpose and a limited time. An example would be a three-month tourist visa. It is advisable to obtain visas before you leave the United States, because you will not be able to obtain visas for some countries once you have departed. Apply directly to the embassy or consulate of each country you plan to visit. You will have to fill out a form, submit pictures, and surrender your passport where the visa will be stamped, so be prepared to wait a few weeks and apply early.

MEDICAL REQUIREMENTS IN FOREIGN COUNTRIES

Some countries may also require medical vaccinations. The consulate would be a good place to check. A letter from your doctor, describing preexisting medical problems, including information on prescription medicines you take, may come in handy for customs processing. You should also have the generic names of the drugs and leave them in their original, labeled containers. If you have allergies, reactions to certain medicines, or any other unique medical problems, consider wearing a medical alert bracelet or carrying a similar warning.

If you become seriously ill or injured overseas, obtaining medical treatment and hospital care can be costly. The Social Security/ Medicare program does not cover hospital and medical services outside the United States. Before you leave the United States learn what medical services your health insurance will cover abroad. If your health insurance policy does not cover you abroad, you should purchase a temporary health policy that does. There are several short-term health and emergency assistance policies designed for travelers. For further information contact your travel or insurance agent. Consider a plan that covers bringing you home for treatment as well, because that can cost as much as $5,000, depending on your location and condition.

PROTECTING YOUR VALUABLES

Safeguard your money while travelling. Nothing can take the fun out of sight-seeing faster than a stolen wallet. The first rule is, Do not carry large amounts of cash. Take most of your money in traveler's checks and remember to record the serial number, denomination, date, and location of the issuing bank. Keep this information in a safe place separate from your valuables. Record the numbers of the credit cards you take with you and keep the list separate from the cards. Leave all unnecessary credit cards at home. Before departing, you may wish to purchase small amounts of foreign currency to use for buses, taxis, phones, or tips when you first arrive. You can purchase foreign currency at some banks, foreign exchange firms, or windows and vending machines at many international airports.

If you intend to drive overseas, check with the embassy or consulate of the countries you will visit to learn of their driver's license, road permit, and auto insurance requirements. Many countries do not recognize a U.S. driver's license. Most, however, accept an international driver's permit. The local automobile association can provide you with one but you must be at least eighteen, have two passport-sized photos, and have a valid U.S. license. Some countries require road permits instead of tolls to use their divided highways and will fine drivers without a permit.

Leave a detailed itinerary with names, addresses, and phone numbers of persons and places you will be visiting with relatives or friends in the United States so you can be reached in an emergency. Remember to also include a photocopy of your passport information.

Your trip overseas can provide you with many wonderful memories. However, there are a few things to keep in mind while you are seeing the sights and shopping. Have a reasonable amount of cash with you, but not more than you will need for a day or two. Convert your traveler's checks to a local currency as you use them, rather than all at once. If you must take jewelry or other valuables, use hotel security vaults to store them.

Your passport is the most valuable document you will carry abroad. It confirms your U.S. citizenship. Guard it carefully. Do not use it as collateral for a loan or lend it to anyone. You will probably need it when you pick up mail or check into hotels, embassies, or consulates. It is a good idea to pack an "emergency kit" to help you get a replacement passport in case yours is lost or stolen. To make a kit, obtain the date-page photocopy; write down the addresses and telephone numbers of the U.S. embassies and consulates in the countries you plan to visit; and put this information, along with two-passport-sized photographs, in a place separate from your passport.

While on the streets and in restaurants guard against theft. Coat pockets, handbags, and hip pockets are particularly susceptible to theft. Thieves will use all kinds of ploys to divert your attention just long enough to pick your pocket and grab your purse or wallet. These ploys include creating a disturbance, spilling something on your clothing, and many others. Consider not carrying a purse or wallet when going on to crowded streets. Women who carry a shoulder bag should keep it tucked under the arm and held securely. Men should put their wallets in their front trouser pockets or use money belts. Be especially cautious in a large crowd in the subway, marketplace, or even at a festival.

Buying Merchandise in Foreign Countries

When shopping beware of purchasing souvenirs made from endangered wildlife. These species and products made from them are prohibited either by U.S. or foreign laws from import into the United States. Prohibited products include ivory, furs from spotted cats or marine animals, products from sea turtles, feathers from wild birds, many live and stuffed birds, most crocodile and caiman leather, and most coral and coral jewelry. Your wildlife souvenirs could be confiscated by the government inspectors, and you could face other penalties for attempting to bring them into the United States.

Be cautious of buying glazed ceramic-ware abroad. It is possible to suffer lead poisoning if you consume food or beverages that are stored or served in improperly glazed ceramics. The U.S. Food and Drug Administration recommends that ceramic tableware purchased abroad be tested for lead release by a commercial laboratory on your return or be used for decorative purposes only.

For you antique lovers, some countries consider antiques to be national treasures and the "inalienable property of the nation." In these and other countries, customs authorities will seize illegally purchased antiques without compensation and may also levy fines on the purchaser. If you have questions about purchasing antiques, the country's tourist office can guide you.

Keep all receipts for items you buy overseas. They will be helpful in making your U.S. Customs declaration when you return.

Obeying Foreign Laws and Regulations

While abroad, you are subject to the laws and regulations of your host country and are not protected by the U.S. Constitution and laws. Try to avoid areas of unrest and disturbance. Deal only with authorized outlets when exchanging money or buying airline tickets and traveler's checks. Do not deliver a package for anyone unless you know the person well and are certain the package does not contain drugs or other contraband. Keep in mind that many countries have stiff penalties for drug violations and strictly enforce drug laws. If you should be detained by local authorities, ask to talk to a U.S. consular officer. Under international agreements and practice, you have a right to contact an American consul. Although U.S. consuls cannot act as your attorney or get you out of jail, they can provide you with a list of local attorneys and inform you of your rights under local laws.

Should you encounter serious legal, medical, or financial difficulties while abroad, contact the nearest U.S. embassy or consulate for assistance. Consular officers cannot cash checks, lend money, or act as travel agents. However, in an emergency, they can help you get funds wired to you and let relatives or friends at home know of your situation. In the case of a death abroad, consular officials will contact the next of kin in the United States and will explain the local requirements. It is a worthwhile precaution to have insurance that covers the cost of local burial or shipment of remains home. Otherwise, this cost must be borne by next of kin and can be extremely expensive.

While travelling, you should register at the consular section of the nearest U.S. embassy or consulate in the following situations:

- If you find yourself in a country or area that is experiencing civil unrest, has an unstable political climate, or is undergoing a natural disaster, such as an earthquake or hurricane
- If you plan to go to a country where there are no U.S. officials. In such cases, register in an adjacent country, leave an

itinerary, and ask about what third country may represent U.S. interests there.

- If you plan to stay in a country for longer than one month.

RETURNING TO THE UNITED STATES

On your return trip home reconfirm your reservation at least seventy-two hours before departure. Whenever possible, obtain a written confirmation. If you do it by phone, record the time, day, and the agent's name who took the call. Some countries levy an airport departure tax on travelers that can be $50 or more. Ask the airline or travel agent for details, and make certain you have enough money at the end of your trip to be able to get on the plane.

Have your passport ready when you go through immigration and customs. Also have your receipts handy in case you need to support your customs declaration. You should pack your baggage in a way to make inspection easier. For example, pack the articles you acquired abroad separately. U.S. Customs generally allows each U.S. citizen to bring back $400 worth of merchandise duty free. The next $1,000 worth of items brought back for personal use or gifts is subject to duty at a flat rate of 10 percent. For many countries in the Caribbean and Central America the duty-free exemption is $600. For the U.S. Virgin Islands, American Samoa, and Guam, the exemption is $1,200.

There is no limit on the amount of money or negotiable instruments which can be brought into or taken out of the United States. However, any amount over $10,000 must be reported to the U.S. Customs when you depart or enter the country. Do not bring home any fresh fruit or vegetables because they may be confiscated.

If you encounter problems during your trip with the tour operator, airlines, hotel, or others, try to resolve it on the spot rather than wait. If your complaint does not get resolved immediately, at least you will have registered your grievance. Keep notes that include the names of the people with whom you speak and the date, time, and location of your conversations. Keep all receipts if you have to spend money to resolve a problem. If your baggage is lost or delayed, file a claim immediately to protect your rights. Be sure to obtain and retain a copy of the claim.

Should you have to pursue a complaint after returning from your trip, first review the materials you were given by the travel agent or supplier. If you are satisfied that your complaint has merit, write a letter to the firm that you feel is responsible. Outline the nature of your complaint, as well as the steps you feel should be taken to rectify the problem. Include copies of supporting documentation. You should also seek the assistance of your travel agent, who will often pursue the matter for you. If you are unable to get satisfactory response to your complaint, you should contact a Better Business Bureau, government consumer affairs office, American Society of Travel Agents, United States Tour Operators Association, or a lawyer if necessary.

Travel during your senior years can be one of your most enjoyable and enriching pastimes. To ensure against problems, do your homework, plan early, and follow the guidelines discussed earlier in this chapter.

Bon Voyage!

APPENDIX A: SELECTED FEDERAL AGENCIES

THE FOLLOWING FEDERAL AGENCIES PROVIDE SERVICES AND resources to retirees, senior citizens, and consumers.

Commission on Civil Rights
1121 Vermont Avenue, N.W., Suite 800
Washington, DC 20425
(800) 552-6843 *(toll-free complaint referral outside DC)*
(202) 376-8512 *(complaint referral in DC)*

Consumer Information Center (CIC)
Pueblo, CO 81009
You can obtain a free Consumer Information Catalog by writing to the above address or by calling (719) 948-4000.

Department of Agriculture
Office of the Consumer Advisor
Washington, DC 20250
(202) 382-9681

Department of Commerce
Office of Consumer Affairs, Room 5718
Washington, DC 20230
(202) 377-5001

Department of Defense
Office of National Ombudsman
National Committee for Employer Support of the Guard and Reserve
1555 Wilson Boulevard, Suite 200
Arlington, VA 22209-2405
(703) 696-1400; 1 (800) 336-4590 *(toll-free outside DC metropolitan area)*
Provides assistance with employer/employee problems for members of the Guard and Reserve and their employers.

Department of Education
Clearinghouse on Disability Information
OSERS
Room 330 C Street, S.W.
Washington, DC 20202-2524
(202) 732-1241

Department of Energy
Office of Consumer and Public Liaison
Washington, DC 20585
(202) 586-5373

Food and Drug Administration (FDA)
Look in your telephone directory under "U.S. Government, Health and Human Services Department, Food and Drug Administration"

Department of Health and Human Services
AIDS Hotline (Acquired Immune Deficiency Syndrome)
(800) 342-AIDS *(toll-free)*

Department of Health and Human Services
Cancer Hotline
(800) 4-CANCER *(toll-free)*

Department of Health and Human Services
Consumer Affairs and Information Staff
Food and Drug Administration
(HFE-88)
5600 Fishers Lane, Room 16085
Rockville, MD 20857
(301) 443-3170

Department of Health and Human Services
Division of Beneficiary Services
Health Care Financing Administration (HCFA)
6325 Security Boulevard
Baltimore, MD 21207
(800) 638-6833 *(toll-free)*

Department of Health and Human Services
National Health Information Center
P.O. Box 1133
Washington, DC 20013-1133
(301) 565-4167 *(Washington Metro Area)*; 1 (800) 336-4797 *(toll-free)*

Department of Health and Human Services
Social Security Administration
(800) SSA-1213 *(toll-free)*

Department of Housing and Urban Development
HUD Fraud Hotline
(202) 708-4200; 1 (800) 347-3735 *(toll-free outside DC)*

Department of Housing and Urban Development
Office of Fair Housing and Equal Opportunity
Room 5100
Washington, DC 20410
(800) 424-8590 *(toll-free outside DC)*

Department of the Interior
Consumer Affairs Administrator
Office of the Secretary
Washington, DC 20240
(202) 208-5521

Department of the Interior
National Park Service
Washington, DC 20240
(202) 208-4917

Department of Justice
Antitrust Division
Washington, DC 20530
(202) 514-2401

Department of Justice, Civil Rights Division
Look in your telephone directory under "U.S. Government, Justice Department, Civil Rights Division." If it does not appear, call the appropriate Federal Information Center (FIC) number or contact:

Civil Rights Division
Department of Justice
Washington, DC 20530
(202) 514-2151

Department of Justice, Federal Bureau of Investigation (FBI)
Look inside the front cover of your telephone directory for the number of the nearest FBI office. If it does not appear, look under "U.S. Government, Federal Bureau of Investigation." You may also contact:

Federal Bureau of Investigation
Washington, DC 20535
(202) 324-3000

Department of Justice, Immigration and Naturalization Service
Look in your telephone directory under "U.S. Government, Justice Department, Immigration and Naturalization Service" or contact:

Immigration and Naturalization Service
425 I Street, N.W.
Washington, DC 20536
(202) 514-4316

Department of Labor
Coordinator of Consumer Affairs
Washington, DC 20210
(202) 523-6060 *(general inquiries)*

Department of Labor
Employment Standards Administration
Office of Public Affairs
Washington, DC 20210
(202) 523-8743

Department of Labor, Occupational Safety and Health Administration (OSHA)
Look in your telephone directory under "U.S. Government, Labor Department, Occupational Safety and Health Administration" or contact:

Occupational Safety and Health Administration
Office of Information and Consumer Affairs
Washington, DC 20210
(202) 523-8151

Department of Labor
Pension and Welfare Benefits Administration
Office of Program Services
Washington, DC 20210
(202) 523-8776

Department of State
Overseas Citizen Services
Washington, DC 20520
(202) 647-3666 *(nonemergencies)*; (202) 647-5225 *(emergencies)*

Department of State
Passport Services
Washington Passport Agency
1425 K Street, N.W.
Washington, DC 20524
(202) 647-0518

Department of State
Visa Services
Washington, DC 20520
(202) 647-0510

Department of Transportation (DOT)
Air Safety:
Federal Aviation Administration (FAA)
Community and Consumer Liaison Division, FAA (APA-200)
Washington, DC 20591
(202) 267-3479/8592; (800) FAA-SURE *(toll-free outside DC)*

Airline Service Complaints:
Office of Intergovernmental and Consumer Affairs (I-25)
Department of Transportation
Washington, DC 20590
(202) 366-2220

Auto Safety Hotline:
National Highway Traffic Safety Administration (NHTSA), (NEF-11)
Department of Transportation
Washington, DC 20690
(202) 366-0123

Department of the Treasury, Comptroller of the Currency
The Comptroller of the Currency handles complaints about national banks, i.e., banks that have the word "National" in their names or the initials "N.A." after their names. For assistance, look in your telephone directory under "U.S. Government, Treasury Department, Comptroller of the Currency" or contact:

Comptroller of the Currency
Director, Compliance Policy
250 E Street, S.W.
Washington, DC 20219
(202) 874-4820

Department of the Treasury, Internal Revenue Service (IRS)
Look in your telephone directory under "U.S. Government, Treasury Department, Internal Revenue Service."

Department of the Treasury, Office of Thrift Supervision
Formerly known as the Federal Home Loan Bank Board, the Office of Thrift Supervision handles complaints about savings and loan associations and savings banks. For assistance contact:

Office of Thrift Supervision
Consumer Affairs
1700 G Street, N.W.
Washington, DC 20552
(202) 906-6237; (800) 842-6929 *(toll-free outside DC)*

Department of the Treasury
United States Savings Bonds Division
Office of Public Affairs
Washington, DC 20220
(202) 634-5389; (800) US-BONDS

Department of Veterans Affairs (VA)
For information about VA medical care or benefits, write, call, or visit your nearest VA facility. Your telephone directory will list a VA medical center or regional office under "U.S. Government, Department of Veterans Affairs," or under "U.S. Government, Veterans Administration." You may also contact the offices listed below.

For information about benefits:
Veterans Benefits Administration (27)
Department of Veterans Affairs
810 Vermont Avenue, N.W.
Washington, DC 20420
(202) 233-2576

For information about medical care:
Veterans Health Administration (184C)
810 Vermont Avenue, N.W.
Washington, DC 20420
(202) 535-7208

For consumer information or general assistance:
Consumer Affairs Service
Department of Veterans Affairs
810 Vermont Avenue, N.W.
Washington, DC 20420
(202) 535-8962

Federal Communications Commission (FCC)
Complaints about telephone systems:
Common Carrier Bureau
Informal Complaints Branch
Federal Communications Commission
1919 M Street, N.W., Room 6202
Washington, DC 20554
(202) 632-7553

General information:
Consumer Assistance and Small Business Office
Federal Communications Commission
1919 M Street, N.W., Room 254
Washington, DC 20554
(202) 632-7000

Complaints about radio or television:
Mass Media Bureau
Complaints and Investigations
Federal Communications Commission
2025 M Street, N.W., Room 8210
Washington, DC 20554
(202) 632-7048

Federal Deposit Insurance Corporation (FDIC)
FDIC handles questions about deposit insurance coverage and complaints about FDIC-insured state banks that are not members of the Federal Reserve System. For assistance, look in your telephone directory under "U.S. Government, Federal Deposit Insurance Corporation" or contact:

Office of Consumer Affairs
Federal Deposit Insurance Corporation
550 17th Street, N.W.
Washington, DC 20429
(202) 898-3536; (800) 424-5588 *(toll-free outside DC)*

Federal Reserve System
The Board of Governors handles consumer complaints about state-chartered banks and trust companies that are members of the Federal Reserve System. For assistance, look in your telephone directory under "U.S. Government, Federal Reserve System, Board of Governors," or "Federal Reserve Bank" or contact:

Board of Governors of the Federal Reserve System
Division of Consumer and Community Affairs
Washington, DC 20551
(202) 452-3946

Federal Trade Commission (FTC)
Look in your telephone directory under "U.S. Government, Federal Trade Commission" or contact:

Correspondence Branch
Federal Trade Commission
Washington, DC 20580

Public Reference Section
Federal Trade Commission
6th and Pennsylvania Ave., N.W., Room 130
Washington, DC 20580
(202) 326-2222 *(publications)*

Government Publications:
Government Printing Office (GPO)
Publications Service Section
Government Printing Office
Washington, DC 20402
(202) 275-3050

Interstate Commerce Commission
Office of Compliance and Consumer Assistance
Washington, DC 20423
(202) 275-7148

National Credit Union Administration
Look in your telephone directory under "U.S. Government, National Credit Union Administration" or contact:

National Credit Union Administration
1776 G Street, N.W.
Washington, DC 20456
(202) 682-9640

National Labor Relations Board
Office of the Executive Secretary
1717 Pennsylvania Ave., N.W., Room 701
Washington, DC 20570
(202) 254-9430

Pension Benefit Guaranty Corporation
2020 K Street, N.W.
Washington, DC 20006-1860
(202) 778-8800

Consumer Advocate
Postal Rate Commission
1333 H Street, N.W., Suite 300
Washington, DC 20268
(202) 789-6830

President's Committee on Employment of People with Disabilities
1111 20th Street, N.W., Suite 636
Washington, DC 20036-3470
(202) 653-5044

Railroad Retirement Board
844 Rush Street
Chicago, IL 60611
(312) 751-4500

Securities and Exchange Commission (SEC)
Office of Filings, Information, and Consumer Services
450 5th Street, N.W.
(Mail Stop 2-6)
Washington, DC 20549
(202) 272-7440 *(investor complaints)*; (202) 272-5624 *(SEC Information Line: general topics and sources of assistance)*

Small Business Administration (SBA)
Office of Consumer Affairs
409 Third Street, N.W.
Washington, DC 20416
(202) 205-6948 *(complaints only)*; (800) U-ASK-SBA *(toll-free information)*

U.S. Consumer Product Safety Commission (CPSC)
To report a hazardous product or a product-related injury, or to inquire about product recalls, call or write:

U.S. Consumer Product Safety Commission
Product Safety Hotline
Washington, DC 20207
(800) 638-CPSC *(toll-free; complaints only)*

United States Postal Service
If you experience difficulty when ordering merchandise or conducting business transactions through the mail, or suspect that you have been the victim of a mail fraud or misrepresentation scheme, contact your postmaster or local postal inspector. Look in your telephone directory under "U.S. Government, Postal Service" for these local listings or contact:

Chief Postal Inspector
United States Postal Service
Washington, DC 20260-2100
(202) 268-4267

For consumer convenience, all post offices and letter carriers have postage-free consumer service cards available for reporting mail problems and submitting comments and suggestions. If the problem cannot be resolved using the Consumer Service Card or through direct contact with the local post office, write or call:

Consumer Advocate
United States Postal Service
Washington, DC 20260-6720
(202) 268-2284

APPENDIX B: STATE GOVERNMENT CONSUMER PROTECTION OFFICES

THE FOLLOWING STATE CONSUMER PROTECTION AGENCIES ARE sources of valuable consumer information and assistance in handling consumer complaints.

Alabama
Consumer Protection Division
Office of Attorney General
11 South Union Street
Montgomery, AL 36130
(205) 242-7334; (800) 392-5658 *(toll-free in AL)*

Arizona
Consumer Protection
Office of the Attorney General
1275 West Washington Street, Room 259
Phoenix, AZ 85007
(602) 542-3702; (602) 542-5763 *(consumer information and complaints)*;
(800) 352-8431 *(toll-free in AZ)*

Consumer Protection
Office of the Attorney General
402 West Congress Street, Suite 315
Tucson, AZ 85701
(602) 628-6504

Arkansas
Consumer Protection Division
Office of Attorney General
200 Tower Building
323 Center Street
Little Rock, AR 72201
(800) 482-8982

California
California Dept of Consumer Affairs
400 R Street, Suite 1040
Sacramento, CA 95814
(916) 445-0660 *(complaint assistance)*; (916) 445-1254 *(consumer information)*; (916) 522-1799 *(TDD)*; (800) 344-9940 *(toll-free in CA)*

Office of Attorney General
Public Inquiry Unit
P.O. Box 944255
Sacramento, CA 94244-2550
(916) 322-3360; (800) 952-5225 *(toll-free in CA)*; (800) 952-5548 *(toll-free TDD in CA)*

Bureau of Automotive Repair
California Dept of Consumer Affairs
10240 Systems Parkway
Sacramento, CA 95827
(916) 366-5100; (800) 952-5210 *(toll-free in CA; auto repair only)*

Colorado
Consumer Protection Unit
Office of Attorney General
110 16th Street, 10th Floor
Denver, CO 80202
(303) 620-4500

Consumer and Food Specialist
Department of Agriculture
700 Kipling Street, Suite 4000
Lakewood, CO 80215-5894
(303) 239-4114

Delaware
Division of Consumer Affairs
Department of Community Affairs
820 North French Street, 4th Floor
Wilmington, DE 19801
(302) 577-3250

Economic Crime and Consumer Protection
Office of Attorney General
820 North French Street
Wilmington, DE 19801
(302) 577-3250

District of Columbia
Department of Consumer and Regulatory Affairs
614 H Street, N.W.
Washington, DC 20001
(202) 727-7000

Florida
Department of Agriculture and Consumer Services
Division of Consumer Services
218 Mayo Building
Tallahassee, FL 32399
(904) 488-2226; (800) 327-3382 *(toll-free information and education in FL)*;
(800) 321-5366 *(toll-free lemon law in FL)*

Consumer Litigation Section
The Capitol
Tallahassee, FL 32399-1050
(904) 488-9105

Consumer Division
Office of Attorney General
4000 Hollywood Boulevard, Suite 505 South
Hollywood, FL 33021
(305) 985-4780

Georgia
Governors Office of Consumer Affairs
2 Martin Luther King, Jr. Drive, S.E.
Plaza Level—East Tower
Atlanta, GA 30334
(404) 651-8600; (404) 656-3790; (800) 869-1123 *(toll-free in GA)*

Hawaii
Office of Consumer Protection
Department of Commerce and Consumer Affairs
828 Fort St. Mall, Suite 2000B
P.O. Box 3767
Honolulu, HI 96812-3767
(808) 586-2630

Idaho
Office of the Attorney General
Consumer Protection Unit
Statehouse, Room 113A
Boise, ID 83720-1000
(208) 334-2424; (800) 432-3545 *(toll-free in ID)*

Illinois
Governor's Office of Citizen's Assistance
222 South College
Springfield, IL 62706
(217) 782-0244; (800) 642-3112 *(toll-free in IL)*

Consumer Protection Division
Office of Attorney General
100 West Randolph, 12th Floor
Chicago, IL 60601
(312) 814-3580; (312) 793-2852 *(TDD)*

Department of Citizen Rights
100 West Randolph, 13th Floor
Chicago, IL 60601
(312) 814-3289

Indiana
Consumer Protection Division
Office of Attorney General
219 State House
Indianapolis, IN 46204
(317) 232-6330; (800) 382-5516 *(toll-free in IN)*

Iowa
Consumer Protection Division
Office of Attorney General
1300 East Walnut Street, 2nd Floor
Des Moines, IA 50319
(515) 261-5926

Kansas
Consumer Protection Division
Office of Attorney General
301 West 10th
Kansas Judicial Center
Topeka, KS 66612-1597
(913) 296-3751; (800) 432-2310 *(toll-free in KS)*

Kentucky
Consumer Protection Division
Office of Attorney General
209 Saint Clair Street
Frankfort, KY 40601-1875
(800) 432-9257 *(toll-free in KY)*

Louisiana
Consumer Protection Section
Office of Attorney General
State Capitol Building
P.O. Box 94005
Baton Rouge, LA 70804-9005
(504) 342-7373

Maine
Superintendent
Bureau of Consumer Credit Protection
State House Station No. 35
Augusta, ME 04333-0035
(207) 582-8718; (800) 332-8529 *(toll-free)*

Consumer and Antitrust Division
Office of Attorney General
State House Station No. 6
Augusta, ME 04333
(207) 289-3716 *(9 A.M.–1 P.M.)*

Maryland
Consumer Protection Division
Office of Attorney General
200 St. Paul Place
Baltimore, MD 21202-2021
(301) 528-8662; (800) 969-5766 *(toll-free)*

Massachusetts
Consumer Protection Division
Department of Attorney General
131 Tremont Street
Boston, MA 02111
(617) 727-8400

Michigan
Consumer Protection Division
Office of Attorney General
P.O. Box 30213
Lansing, MI 48909
(517) 373-1140

Michigan Consumers Council
414 Hollister Building
106 West Allegan Street
Lansing, MI 48933
(517) 373-0947

Minnesota
Office of Consumer Services
Office of Attorney General
117 University Avenue
St. Paul, MN 55155
(612) 296-2331

Mississippi
Consumer Protection Division
Office of Attorney General
P.O. Box 22947
Jackson, MS 39225-2947
(601) 354-6018

Missouri
Office of the Attorney General
Consumer Complaints or Problems
P.O. Box 899
Jefferson City, MO 65102
(314) 751-3321; (800) 392-8222 *(toll-free in MO)*

Montana
Consumer Affairs Unit
Department of Commerce
1424 Ninth Avenue
Helena, MT 59620
(406) 444-4312

Nebraska
Consumer Protection Division
Department of Justice
2115 State Capitol, P.O. Box 98920
Lincoln, NE 68509
(402) 471-2682

Nevada
Commissioner of Consumer Affairs
Department of Commerce
State Mail Room Complex
Las Vegas, NV 89158
(702) 486-7355; (800) 992-0900 *(toll-free in NV)*

New Hampshire
Consumer Protection and Antitrust Bureau
Office of Attorney General
State House Annex
Concord, NH 03301
(603) 271-3641

New Jersey
Division of Consumer Affairs
P.O. Box 45027
Newark, NJ 07101
(201) 648-4010

Department of the Public Advocate
CN 850, Justice Complex
Trenton, NJ 08625
(609) 292-7087; (800) 792-8600 *(toll-free in NJ)*

New Mexico
Consumer Protection Division
Office of Attorney General
P.O. Drawer 1508
Santa Fe, NM 87504
(505) 827-6060; (800) 432-2070 *(toll-free in NM)*

New York
New York State Consumer Protection Board
99 Washington Avenue
Albany, NY 12210-2891
(518) 474-8583

Bureau of Consumer Frauds and Protection
Office of Attorney General
State Capitol
Albany, NY 12224
(518) 474-5481

North Carolina
Consumer Protection Section
Office of Attorney General
Raney Building
P.O. Box 629
Raleigh, NC 27602
(919) 733-7741

Ohio
Consumer Frauds and Crimes Section
Office of Attorney General
20 East Broad Street
State Office Tower, 25th Floor
Columbus, OH 43266-0410
(614) 466-4986 *(complaints)*; (800) 282-0515 *(toll-free in OH)*

Oklahoma
Office of Attorney General
420 West Main, Suite 550
Oklahoma City, OK 73102
(405) 521-4274

Department of Consumer Credit
4545 Lincoln Blvd., Suite 104
Oklahoma City, OK 73105-3408
(405) 521-3653

Oregon
Financial Fraud Section
Department of Justice
Justice Building
Salem, OR 97310
(503) 378-4320

Pennsylvania
Bureau of Consumer Protection
Office of Attorney General
Strawberry Square, 14th Floor
Harrisburg, PA 17120
(717) 787-9707; (800) 441-2555 *(toll-free in PA)*

Puerto Rico
Department of Consumer Affairs (DACO)
Minillas Station, P.O. Box 41059
Santurce, PR 00940
(809) 721-0940

Department of Justice
P.O. Box 192
San Juan, PR 00902
(809) 721-2900

Rhode Island
Consumer Protection Division
Department of Attorney General
72 Pine Street
Providence, RI 02903
(401) 277-2104; (800) 852-7776 *(toll-free in RI)*

Rhode Island Consumers' Council
365 Broadway
Providence, RI 02909
(401) 277-2764

South Carolina
Consumer Fraud and Antitrust Section
Office of Attorney General
P.O. Box 11549
Columbia, SC 29211
(803) 734-3970

Department of Consumer Affairs
P.O. Box 5757
Columbia, SC 29250-5757
(803) 734-9452; (800) 922-1594 *(toll-free in SC)*

South Dakota
Division of Consumer Affairs
Office of Attorney General
500 East Capitol, State Capitol Building
Pierre, SD 57501-5070
(605) 773-4400

Tennessee
Antitrust and Consumer Protection Div.
Office of Attorney General
450 James Robertson Parkway
Nashville, TN 37243-0485
(615) 741-2672

Division of Consumer Affairs
Department of Commerce and Insurance
500 James Robertson Parkway, 5th Floor
Nashville, TN 37243-0600
(615) 741-4737; (800) 342-8385 *(toll-free in TN)*

Texas
Assistant Attorney General and Chief Consumer Protection Division
Office of Attorney General
P.O. Box 12548
Austin, TX 78711
(512) 463-2070

Utah
Division of Consumer Protection
Department of Commerce
160 East 3rd South
P.O. Box 45802
Salt Lake City, UT 84145-0802
(801) 530-6601

Vermont
Public Protection Division
Office of Attorney General
109 State Street
Montpelier, VT 05609-1001
(802) 828-3171

Virginia
Antitrust and Consumer Litigation Section
Office of Attorney General
Supreme Court Building
101 North Eighth Street
Richmond, VA 23219
(804) 786-2116; (800) 451-1525 *(toll-free in VA)*

Division of Consumer Affairs
Department of Agriculture and Consumer Services
Room 101, Washington Building
1100 Bank Street, P.O. Box 1163
Richmond, VA 23219
(804) 786-2042

Washington
Consumer and Business
Fair Practices Division
Office of the Attorney General
111 Olympia Avenue, NE
Olympia, WA 98501
(206) 753-6210

West Virginia
Consumer Protection Division
Office of Attorney General
812 Quarrier Street, 6th Floor
Charleston, WV 25301
(304) 348-8986; (800) 368-8808 *(toll-free in WV)*

Wisconsin
Division of Trade and Consumer Protection
Department of Agriculture, Trade and Consumer Protection
801 West Badger Road, P.O. Box 8911
Madison, WI 53708
(608) 266-9836; (800) 422-7128 *(toll-free in WI)*

Wyoming
Office of Attorney General
123 Capital Building
Cheyenne, WY 82002
(307) 777-7874

APPENDIX C: STATE AGENCIES ON AGING

THE OFFICES LISTED IN THIS SECTION COORDINATE SERVICES FOR older Americans. They provide information on services, programs, and opportunities for these consumers.

Alabama
Commission on Aging
136 Catoma Street
Montgomery, AL 36130
(205) 242-5743; (800) 243-5463
(toll-free in AL)

Alaska
Older Alaskans Commission
P.O. Box C
Juneau, AK 99811-0209

Arizona
Aging and Adult Administration
1400 West Washington, 950A
Phoenix, AZ 85007
(602) 542-4446

Arkansas
Office of Aging and Adult Services
Department of Human Services
P.O. Box 1437
Little Rock, AR 72203-1437
(501) 682-2441; (800) 482-8040
(toll-free in AR)

California
Department of Aging
1600 K Street
Sacramento, CA 95814
(916) 322-5290; (800) 231-4024
(toll-free in CA)

Colorado
Colorado Department of Social Services
1575 Sherman Street
Denver, CO 80203-1714
(303) 866-5700

Connecticut
Department on Aging
175 Main Street
Hartford, CT 06106
(302) 566-3238; (800) 443-9946 *(toll-free in CT)*

Delaware
Department of Health and Social Services
Division of Aging
1908 North DuPont Highway
New Castle, DE 19720
(302) 421-6791; (800) 223-9074 *(toll-free in DE)*

District of Columbia
D.C. Office on Aging
1424 K Street, N.W., 2nd Floor
Washington, DC 20005
(202) 724-5623

Florida
Aging and Adult Services
1321 Winewood Boulevard, Room 323
Tallahassee, FL 32399-0700
(904) 488-8922

Georgia
Office of Aging
878 Peachtree Street, N.E., Suite 632
Atlanta, GA 30309
(404) 894-5333

Hawaii
Executive Office on Aging
335 Merchant Street, Room 241
Honolulu, HI 98613
(808) 548-2593; (800) 468-4644 *(toll-free in HI)*

Idaho
Idaho Office on Aging
Statehouse, Room 108
Boise, ID 83720
(208) 334-3833

Illinois
Department on Aging
421 East Capitol Avenue
Springfield, IL 62701
(217) 785-2870; (800) 252-8966 *(toll-free voice TDD)*

Indiana
Aging/In-Home Care
Services Division
Department of Human Services
P.O. Box 7083
Indianapolis, IN 46207-7083
(317) 232-7020; (800) 622-4972 *(toll-free in IN)*

Iowa
Department of Elder Affairs
914 Grand Avenue, Suite 236
Des Moines, IA 50319
(515) 281-5187; (800) 532-3213 *(toll-free in IA)*

Kansas
Department on Aging
Docking State Office Building, Room 122 S
915 Southwest Harrison Street
Topeka, KS 66612-1500
(913) 296-4986; (800) 432-3535 *(toll-free in KS)*

Kentucky
Division for Aging Services
Department for Social Services
275 East Main Street, 6th Floor West
Frankfort, KY 40621
(502) 564-6930; (800) 372-2991 *(toll-free in KY)*

Louisiana
Governor's Office of Elder Affairs
P.O. Box 80374
Baton Rouge, LA 70898
(504) 925-1700

Maine
Bureau of Elder and Adult Service
35 Anthony Avenue
Statehouse, Station 11
Augusta, ME 04333-0011
(207) 626-5335

Maryland
Office on Aging
301 West Preston Street, 10th Floor
Baltimore, MD 21201
(301) 225-1100; (800) 243-3425 *(toll-free in MD)*

Massachusetts
Executive Office of Elder Affairs
38 Chauncy Street
Boston, MA 02111
(617) 727-7750; (800) 882-2003 *(toll-free in MA)*

Michigan
Office of Services to the Aging
P.O. Box 30026
Lansing, MI 48909
(517) 373-8230

Minnesota
Minnesota Board on Aging
444 Lafayette Road
St. Paul, MN 55155-3843
(800) 652-9747 *(toll-free in MN)*

Mississippi
Divison of Aging and Adult Services
421 West Pascagoula Street
Jackson, MS 39203
(601) 949-2070; (800) 453-6347 *(toll-free in MS)*

Missouri
Division of Aging
P.O. Box 1337
Jefferson City, MO 65102
(314) 751-8535; (800) 392-0210 *(toll-free in MO)*

Montana
Coordinator of Aging Services
Governor's Office
State Capitol
Helena, MT 59620
(406) 444-4204; (800) 332-2272 *(toll-free in MT)*

Nebraska
Nebraska Department on Aging
State Office Building
P.O. Box 95044
Lincoln, NB 68509
(402) 471-2306

Nevada
Division for Aging Services
Department of Human Resources
340 North 11th Street
Las Vegas, NV 89158
(702) 486-3545

New Hampshire
Division of Elderly and Adult Services
6 Hazen Drive
Concord, NH 03301
(603) 271-4680; (800) 351-1888 *(toll-free in NH)*

New Jersey
Division on Aging
Department of Community Affairs
101 South Broad Street, CN 807
Trenton, NJ 08625
(609) 292-4833; (800) 792-8820 *(toll-free in NJ)*

New Mexico
State Agency on Aging
224 East Palace Avenue, 4th Floor
Santa Fe, NM 87501
(800) 432-2080 *(toll-free in NM)*

New York
New York State Office for the Aging
Agency Building 2, ESP
Albany, NY 12223
(518) 474-5731; (800) 342-9871 *(toll-free in NY)*

North Carolina
Division on Aging
Department of Human Resources
Caller Box No. 2953
693 Palmer Drive
Raleigh, NC 27626-0531
(919) 733-3983; (800) 662-7030 *(toll-free in NC)*

North Dakota
Aging Services
Department of Human Services
600 East Boulevard
Bismarck, ND 58505
(701) 224-2310; (800) 472-2622 *(toll-free in ND)*

Ohio
Ohio Department of Aging
50 West Broad Street, 9th Floor
Columbus, OH 43266-0501
(614) 466-5500; (800) 282-1206
(toll-free in OH)

Oklahoma
Special Unit on Aging
P.O. Box 25352
Oklahoma City, OK 73125
(405) 521-2281

Oregon
Senior Services Division
Department of Human Resources
State of Oregon
313 Public Service Building
Salem, OR 97310
(503) 378-4728; (800) 232-3020
(toll-free in OR)

Pennsylvania
Department of Aging
231 State Street
Harrisburg, PA 17101
(717) 783-1549

Puerto Rico
Office of Elder Affairs
Call Box 563
Old San Juan
Station, PR 00902
(809) 721-4560

Rhode Island
Department of Elderly Affairs
160 Pine Street
Providence, RI 02903
(401) 277-2880; (800) 322-2880
(toll-free in RI)

South Carolina
South Carolina Commission on Aging
400 Arbor Lake Drive, Suite B-500
Columbia, SC 29223
(803) 735-0210; (800) 868-9095
(toll-free)

South Dakota
Office of Adult Services and Aging
700 Governors Drive
Pierre, SD 57501
(605) 773-3656

Tennessee
Commission on Aging
706 Church Street, Suite 201
Nashville, TN 37243-0860
(615) 741-2056

Texas
Texas Department on Aging
P.O. Box 12786, Capitol Station
Austin, TX 78711
(512) 444-2727; (800) 252-9240
(toll-free in TX)

Utah
Division of Aging and Adult Services
P.O. Box 45500
Salt Lake City, UT 84145-0500
(801) 538-3910

Vermont
Department of Aging
and Disabilities
103 South Main Street
Waterbury, VT 05671-2301
(802) 241-2400

Virginia
Department for the Aging
700 East Franklin Street, 10th
Floor
Richmond, VA 23219
(804) 225-2271; (800) 552-4464
(toll-free in VA)

Washington
Aging and Adult Services
Administration
OB-44A
Olympia, WA 98504
(206) 493-2509; (800) 422-3263
(toll-free in WA)

West Virginia
Commission on Aging
State Capitol
Charleston, WV 25305
(304) 348-3317

Wisconsin
Bureau on Aging
P.O. Box 7851
Madison, WI 53707
(608) 266-2536

Wyoming
Division on Aging
139 Hathaway Building
Cheyenne, WY 82002-0480
(307) 777-7986; (800) 442-2766
(toll-free in WY)

Appendix D: Other Organizations and Sources of Information

American Association of Retired Persons (AARP)
1909 K Street, N.W.
Washington, DC 20049
(202) 728-4355

American Society of Travel Agents, Inc. (ASTA)
1101 King Street
Alexandria, VA 22314
(703) 739-2782

Consumer Federation of America
1424 Street, N.W., Suite 604
Washington, DC 20036

Direct Selling Association
1730 M Street, N.W., Suite 60
Washington, DC 20036

Institute of Certified Financial Planners
7600 E. Eastman Avenue, Suite 301
Denver, CO 80231
(303) 751-7600

International Association for Financial Planning
2 Concourse Parkway, Suite 800
Atlanta, GA 30328
(404) 395-1605

National Association of Personal Financial Advisors
1130 Lake Cook Rd, Suite 105
Buffalo Grove, IL 60089
(800) 366-2732

National Foundation for
Consumer Credit
8701 Georgia Avenue, Suite 507
Silver Spring, MD 20910
(301) 589-5600

American Council of Life
Insurance (ACLI)
1001 Pennsylvania Avenue, N.W.
Washington, DC 20004-2599
(202) 624-2455

Health Insurance Association of
America (HIAA)
1025 Connecticut Ave., N.W.
Washington, DC 20036-3998
(202) 223-7780

Continental Association of
Funeral and Memorial
Societies, Inc.
7910 Woodmont Avenue
Bethesda, MD 20814
(301) 913-0030

Council of Better Business
Bureaus, Inc.
4200 Wilson Blvd.
Arlington, VA 22203
(703) 276-0100

TRW Credit Information
P.O. Box 74929
Dallas, TX 75374
(714) 991-5100

Trans-Union Credit Information
P.O. Box 7000
North Olmstead, OH 44070
(312) 408-1050

Associated Credit Service
P.O. Box 674422
Houston, TX 77267
(713) 878-1900

OBI-EQUIFAX
P.O. Box 740241
Atlanta, GA 30374
(800) 685-1111

Director, Mail Order Action Line
Service
Direct Marketing Association
6 East 43rd Street
New York, NY 10017
(212) 689-4977

Code Administrator
Direct Selling Association
1730 M Street, N.W., Suite 60
Washington, DC 20036

INDEX

Page numbers in italics refer to worksheets and illustrations.

B

C

N

O

P

Q

R

S

T

Books from Allworth Press

Legal-Wise: Self-Help Legal Guide for Everyone, Third Edition *by Carl W. Battle, Attorney-at-Law* (softcover, 8½ × 11, 208 pages, $18.95)

The Patent Guide: A Friendly Handbook for Protecting and Profiting from Patents *by Carl W. Battle, Attorney-at-Law* (softcover, 6 × 9, 192 pages, $18.95)

The Copyright Guide: A Friendly Handbook for Protecting and Profiting from Copyrights *by Lee Wilson, Attorney-at-Law* (softcover, 6 × 9, 192 pages, $18.95)

Retire Smart *by David and Virginia Cleary* (softcover, 6 × 9, 224 pages, $12.95)

Your Living Trust and Estate Plan: How to Maximize Your Family's Assets and Protect Your Loved Ones *by Harvey J. Platt Attorney-at-Law* (softcover, 6 × 9, 256 pages, $14.95)

How to Start and Succeed as an Artist *by Daniel Grant* (softcover, 6 × 9, 224 pages, $18.95)

Hers: The Wise Woman's Guide to Starting a Business on $2,000 or Less Revised Edition *By Carol Milano* (softcover, 6 × 9, 224 pages, $16.95)

The Secret Life of Money: How Money Can Be Food for the Soul *by Tad Crawford* (softcover, 5½ × 8½ , 304 pages, $14.95)

Old Money: The Mythology of Wealth in America *by Tad Crawford* (softcover, 6 × 9, 340 pages, $16.95)

Once in Golconda: A True Drama of Wall Street 1920–1938 *by John Brooks* Introduction *by Tad Crawford* (hardcover, 5½ × 8½, 320 pages, $21.95)

The Go-Go Years: The Drama and Crashing Finale of Wall Street's Bullish 60s *by John Brooks* (hardcover, 6¾ × 9½, 392 pages, $24.95)

The Law (in Plain English)® for Small Businesses *by Leonard DuBoff* (softcover, 6 × 9, 256 pages, $19.95)

Licensing Art & Design, Revised Edition *by Caryn R. Leland* (softcover, 6 × 9, 128 pages, $16.95)

Mastering Black-and-White Photography: From Camera to Darkroom *by Bernhard J Suess* (softcover, 6¾ × 10, 240 pages, $18.95)

SOUTHEASTERN COMMUNITY
COLLEGE LIBRARY
WHITEVILLE, NC 28472

Please write to request our free catalog. To order by credit card, call 1-800-491-2808 or send a check or money order to Allworth Press, 10 East 23rd Street, Suite 210, New York, NY 10010. Include $5 for shipping and handling for the first book ordered and $1 for each additional book or $10 plus $1 for each additional book if ordering from Canada. New York State residents must add sales tax.

If you would like to see our complete catalogue on the World Wide Web, you can find us at ***www.allworth.com***